P9-CMT-578

Dr. DOBSON

Turning Hearts Toward Home

The Life and Principles of America's Family Advocate

by
Rolf Zettersten

WORD PUBLISHING
Dallas · London · Sydney · Singapore

Library of Congress Cataloging-in-Publication Data:

Zettersten, Rolf, 1955–
    Dr. Dobson: turning hearts toward home / Rolf Zettersten.
        p.   cm.
    ISBN 0-8499-0525-7
    1. Dobson, James, C., 1936–   . 2. Christian biography—United States.   3. Child psychologists—United States—Biography.
    4. Family—United States.   5. Family—Religious life.   I. Title.
    II. Title: Doctor Dobson.
    BR1725.D62Z48   1989
    269'.2'092—dc20
    [B]   89-39308
                                      CIP

9 8 0 1 2 3 9 RRD 9 8 7 6 5 4 3 2 1

Printed in the United States of America

Contents

I dedicate these pages to my beloved wife, Linda, and our children, Peter and Viveca. This book would have been impossible without their support, encouragement, . . . and patience!

Acknowledgments

I gratefully acknowledge the contributions of many friends and colleagues who shared in the creation of this project. It was truly a team effort, and I sincerely offer my thanks to:

• Dr. James and Shirley Dobson who opened a window into their lives. I pray that others will be drawn closer to Christ, as I have been, through greater familiarity with this special couple.

• Bob and Jan Screen, Chris and Shanon Christian, and Richard and Anne Drumheller who provided me with quiet retreats where these pages were written.

• Maeta Goodwin, Jeanne Pearl, Teresa Watts, Diane Passno, Dee Otte, and Tim Jones—members of the Focus family who gave personal time to help me in a variety of ways.

• Carol Bartley, Dennis Hill, David Moberg, Kip Jordon, Ernie Owen, Byron Williamson, and so many other hard-working people at Word, Inc.

I thank my God upon every remembrance of you!   (Phil. 1:3)

1

The Rest of the Story

In late June 1989 I had an afternoon appointment with Dr. James Dobson in his office at Focus on the Family. I arrived to find him sitting at his desk with red eyes and moist cheeks. My first thought was that something terrible had happened, but I soon learned that he was quietly grieving about the departure of his son, Ryan, the day before. At eighteen years of age, Ryan had graduated from high school and was on his way to a college more than two thousand miles from home. The Dobson nest was suddenly empty, and Jim and Shirley were taking it hard. Then Dr. Dobson showed me a letter he had written to express the depths of his soul. These were his words:

Twenty-three precious years have come and gone since the morning of October 6, 1965, when our first child came into the world. An instant and irrational love affair was born that day between this new dad and his baby daughter, Danae Ann, who took center stage in the Dobson household. How deeply I loved that little girl! She would stand in the doorway each morning and cry as I left for work, and then run giggling and breathless to meet me at the end of the day. You would have thought we had been separated for months. Could I ever love another child as much as this one? I wondered.

Then five years later a little lad named James Ryan made his grand

1

entrance, and it all happened again. He was my boy—the only son I would ever be privileged to raise. What a joy it was to watch him grow and develop and learn. How proud I was to be his father—to be trusted with the well-being of his soul. I put him to bed every night when he was small, and we laughed and we played and we talked about Jesus. I would hide his sister's stuffed animals around the house, and then we would turn out the lights and hunt them with flashlights and a toy rifle. He never tired of that simple game. But the day for games has passed.

This morning, you see, marked the official beginning of the "empty nest" for Shirley and me. Danae graduated from college a year ago and is now building an exciting life of her own. It was difficult for us to let her go, back in 1983, but we took comfort in Ryan's six remaining years at home. How quickly those months have flown, and today, our formal years of parenthood came suddenly to an end. We took Ryan to the airport and sent him off to Colorado for a five-week summer program. Then in August, he plans to enter his freshman year at a college in the Midwest. Though he will be home periodically for years to come, our relationship will not be the same. It might be even better, but it will certainly be different. And I have never liked irreversible change.

Though for many years I knew this moment was coming, and though I had helped others cope with similar experiences, I admit freely that Ryan's departure hit me hard. For the past two weeks, we have worked our way through a massive accumulation of junk in his room. Ryan is a collector of things no one else would want—old street signs, broken models, and favorite fishing rods. The entire family took tetanus shots, and we plunged into the debris. Finally last night, Shirley and Ryan packed the remaining boxes and emptied the last drawer. The job was finished. His suitcases were packed. Our son was ready to go.

Ryan came into my study about midnight, and we sat down for another of the late-night chats that I have cherished. He has always liked to talk at the end of the day. I won't tell you what we said in that final conversation. It is too personal to share with anyone. I can only say that the morning came too quickly, and we drove as a family to the airport. There I was, driving down the freeway, when an unexpected wave of grief swept over me. I thought I couldn't stand to see him go. It was not that I dreaded or didn't look forward to what the future held. No, I mourned the end of an era—a precious time of my life when our children were young and their voices rang in the halls of our house. I couldn't hide the tears as we hugged good-bye at Gate 18. Then Shirley and I drove alone to our house, where a beloved son and daughter had grown from babies to young adults. There I lost it again!

The house that we had left three hours earlier in a whirlwind of activity had been transformed in our absence. It had become a monastery—a morgue—a museum. The silence was deafening to us both. Every corner of it held a memory that wafted through the air. I meandered to Ryan's room and sat on the floor by his bed. His crib had once stood on that spot. Though many years had passed, I could almost see him as a toddler—running and jumping to my open arms. What a happy time that was in my life. The ghost of a kindergartner was there, too, with his brand-new cowboy clothes and his Snoopy lunch pail. Those images are vivid in my mind today. Then a seven-year-old boy appeared before me. He was smiling, and I noticed that his front teeth were missing. His room was filled with bugs and toads and a tarantula named Pebber. As I reached out to hug him, he quietly disappeared. Then a gangly teenager strolled through the door and threw his books on his desk. He looked at me as if to say, "Come on, Dad. Pull yourself together!"

My own words now come back to mind. I remember saying in my second film series, *Turn Your Heart Toward Home,* that the day was coming soon when "the bicycle tires would be flat, the skateboard would be warped and standing in the garage, the swing set would be still, and the beds would not be slept in. We will go through Christmas with no stockings hanging by the fireplace, and the halls will be very quiet. I know those times will soon be here, and I realize it has to be so. I accept it. I wouldn't for anything try to hold back our son or daughter when it comes time to go. But that will also be a very sad day because the precious experience of parenting will have ended for me." Alas, the day that I anticipated has just arrived.

If you're thinking that I am hopelessly sentimental about my kids, you're right. The greatest thrill of my life has been the privilege of raising them day by day in the service of the Lord. Still, I did not expect such intense pain at the time of Ryan's departure. I thought I was prepared to handle the moment, but I quickly realized just how vulnerable I am to the people I love.

In a large sense, however, it is not merely the end of formal parenting that has shaken my world today. I grieve for the human condition itself. When Ryan boarded that plane in Los Angeles, I comprehended anew the brevity of life and the temporary nature of all things. As I sat on the

3

floor in his room, I heard not only Ryan's voice but the voices of my mother and father who laughed and loved in that place. Now they are gone. One day Shirley and I will join them. First one and then the other. We are just "passing through," as the gospel songwriters used to say. All of life boils down to a series of happy "hellos" and sad "good-byes." Nothing is really permanent, not even the relationships that blossom in a healthy home. In time, we must release our grip on everything we hold dear. King David said it best, "As for man, his days are as grass: as a flower of the field, so he flourisheth. For the wind passeth over it, and it is gone; and the place thereof shall know it no more." Yes. I felt the chilly breeze of change blowing through my home this morning, and I understood its meaning.

What an incredibly important scriptural concept this is. If we really grasped the numbering of our days, we would surely be motivated to invest ourselves in eternal values. Would a fifty-year-old man pursue an adulterous affair if he knew how quickly he would stand before his God? Would a woman make herself sick from in-law conflict or other petty frustrations if she knew how little time was left to her? Would men and women devote their lives to the pursuit of wealth and symbols of status if they realized how soon their possessions would be torn from their trembling hands? It is the illusion of permanence, you see, that distorts our perception and shapes our selfish behavior. When eternal values come in view, our greatest desire is to please the Lord and influence as many of our loved ones for Him as possible.

I ask each of my readers this important question. If we really believed that the eternal souls of our children hung in the balance today—that only by winning them for Christ could we spend eternity together in heaven—would we change the way this day is lived? Would we ignore and neglect so great an opportunity if our eyes were fully opened to this awesome responsibility? I think not. I pray not.

Addressing myself now to the mothers and fathers of young children, I urge you to keep this eternal perspective in view as you race through the days of your lives. Don't permit yourselves to become discouraged with the responsibilities of parenting. Yes, it is an exhausting and difficult assignment, and there are times when you will feel like throwing in the towel. But I beg you to stay the course! Get on your knees before the Lord and ask for His strength and wisdom. Finish the job to which He has called you! There is no more important task in living, and you will understand that assignment more clearly when you stand where Shirley and I are today. In the blink of an eye, you will be hugging your children good-bye and returning to an empty house. That is the way the system works.

God bless you all. I love you in the name of Christ.

Sincerely,

James C. Dobson

PS Dear Danae & Ryan

Call home!!

Love, Dad

This letter captures the essence of Dr. James Dobson and explains in part why he is appreciated by millions of people around the world. His great love for his family and for his fellowman is a breath of fresh air in a sterile, high-tech society that has forgotten how to feel. Here is a "man's man" who is not afraid to reveal his passion, his vulnerability, and at times, his sorrow. Here, too, is a rare psychologist who understands eternal priorities and teaches us by personal illustration how to apply them in our lives.

There is another dimension to Dobson's work that helps explain the loyalty of his following. He possesses the unique ability to feel what others are feeling and to give expression to their own longings and anxieties. As such, he offers a life preserver for those who are struggling valiantly to keep their beleaguered families from going under. In a world that is increasingly hostile to Judeo-Christian values, he has never wavered in his defense of the traditional approach to marriage and parenthood. He has stood like a powerful beacon for all the good people who could easily have run aground in the darkness. And believe me, they love him for it. That's why it is not unusual for Dobson to be hugged in restaurants and airports by misty-eyed "friends" who stop to tell him of their appreciation.

But there is more to the story of James Dobson than has been told to date. Having served as vice-president of Focus on the Family for many years, I have found myself in a unique position to observe this man at close range—in unguarded moments, in lengthy meetings, in times of crisis. I'm beginning to understand the principles that have guided his life and the motivation that propels him. That is why I concluded years ago that this "inside look" should be made public. Indeed, I decided to seek Dr. Dobson's approval for such a project.

The first time we discussed the possibility of my writing this book was April 21, 1983. We were walking across the parking lot outside McNichols Arena in Denver, Colorado, where he was scheduled to speak the following evening. As we approached the entrance, I gingerly introduced the idea I had been considering for some time.

"I really think I should write an authorized biography about you and the principles in which you believe," I said.

His response was immediate and predictable. "Man, who would want to read about that?" he asked. "My life has been tame compared to many others'. How could you hold anyone's interest trying to describe me? I wasn't rescued from a life of crime. I never messed around with drugs. I wasn't an all-star athlete. Why, I didn't even rebel against my parents. There's no story there, Rolf. I'm just an ordinary guy."

That was the extent of our conversation, but Dobson's rebuff did not dissuade me. I knew he wouldn't be able to comprehend why anyone would be interested in him. Still, I couldn't help wondering what other "ordinary guy" could affect a generation of his contemporaries, sell millions of books, and draw tens of thousands to hear him speak. I was mulling over that thought when we entered the immense arena and gazed upward at the empty seats that surrounded us.

Dr. Dobson's voice broke my train of thought. "How on earth did I let you guys talk me into booking this arena?" he asked. "I can see it now. Tomorrow night I'll be standing at the podium in front of an empty auditorium. My voice will be bouncing off the distant walls as I say, 'Good evening, friends. Why don't all twenty-five of you make your way down here and join my family on the first row?'"

We enjoyed a good chuckle over his self-effacing humor, but

there was a nervous edge to our laughter. McNichols Arena has a seating capacity of more than nineteen thousand, and professional promoters have had a tough time filling it for rock concerts and sporting events. At this moment Dr. Dobson was certainly justified in feeling "ordinary" as he considered the possibility of a sparse crowd in that huge arena the following evening.

Of course, it was too late to change venues now. He would have to tough it out. Besides, the local committee of volunteers was confident they could do what the professionals could not. Every seat would be occupied, they promised.

The next night Dr. Dobson waited with his wife, Shirley, in a small room offstage to find out if his Denver friends were right. Thirty minutes before starting time, he received his first report. Thousands of people were pouring into the arena, and cars were backed up as far as the eye could see. In fact, a massive traffic jam ensued, delaying the event for almost an hour.

Eventually, every seat was occupied, including those with obstructed views at the upper levels. The arena manager told me it was the first time a speaker had ever drawn nineteen thousand paying customers to his coliseum. "Even the rock star Prince didn't have a sellout when he was here a few months ago," he exclaimed. "Who is this Dobson, anyway?"

Bill Hoskokawa, chief of the *Denver Post*'s editorial page, answered that question two days later. Here is a portion of his Sunday column published April 24, 1983.

Until last week, I hadn't heard of Jim Dobson, although he is a best-selling author and he must be among the nation's best-known radio personalities. Dobson, it turned out, is a tall, athletic, clean-cut, three-piece-suit guru of decency, wholesome family life and loving one's children without pampering them.

That's not as simplistically goody-goody as it may seem. There appears to be a national hungering for his message, and he brings it to millions through a nonprofit organization called Focus on the Family, headquartered in Southern California.

Dr. Dobson (a Ph.D.) and his wife, Shirley, were in Denver last week for an appearance that filled McNichols Sports Arena at $6 a person. But the day before, a local committee made up of people who believed in what Dobson has to say invited upwards of a thousand Denver area businessmen to hear him after lunch at the Marriott downtown.

7

Dobson's message to the businessmen was that while they were making a success of their economic lives, time was speeding by and they ought to be reaching out to humanity, beginning with their own families. It was a simple message, but provocative and challenging.

So swiftly do times change, he said, that most of us do not realize what is happening until one day we discover the kids have grown up and gone, and we've lost forever opportunities to give them a hug and express our love for them. Make the most of the present, he urged, for your relationship with your loved ones will never be the same again.

Of course, we who are privileged to be parents know all this. But sometimes it is important to be reminded by someone as articulate as Jim Dobson.

When he completed his low-key anecdotal address, tough, pragmatic businessmen who had hung on his words gave him a standing ovation.

In more recent years Dobson's influence has continued to escalate. He is now heard daily on more than 1,425 radio stations in twenty-five countries, exceeded in number only by Paul Harvey. He has written eleven books on various aspects of family life, each a best seller in its time. In all, more than six million of his books have been sold.

Three U.S. presidents have sought his assistance (Jimmy Carter, Ronald Reagan, and George Bush), requesting that he serve, in turn, in the fight against juvenile delinquency, teen pregnancy, child abduction, and violent, hard-core pornography. The former chief of staff of the U.S. Army, General John Wickham, appointed him as chairman of the army's Family Initiative. And four universities have awarded him honorary doctoral degrees. The list of accomplishments is seemingly endless, and few could blame James Dobson if he were to become a bit big-headed these days.

But the man has a characteristic modesty that prevents him from seeing himself as others do. According to his wife, Shirley, this is the prayer he offered a few hours before speaking to fifteen thousand people in the Seattle Coliseum: "Lord, the people who have come to hear us are likely to perceive us as celebrities and superstars. But we know what *You* know . . . that we are just a couple of college kids who fell in love, were married, and whom you chose to bless. Help us reach out to all these hurting people tonight." Those are genuine sentiments that help to explain why his colleagues and associates have persuaded James Dobson to allow this book to be written.

Paul Nelson, Focus on the Family's executive vice-president, offered this perspective: "When you work side by side with someone, you have the opportunity to view him as though you were seeing his reflection in one of those magnified makeup mirrors. When you turn on the lights, you see every pore, every whisker, every blemish. Those of us who work closely with Dr. Dobson have looked into that mirror, and we have seen fairness, integrity, understanding, and compassion."

When I first began working with Dobson in 1981, I was skeptical that he could withstand such scrutiny. I had become disillusioned by the hypocrisy I had witnessed in other Christian leaders, and I wondered if any of them lived with integrity. Like so many believers, I knew more than one pastor who had run off with the church secretary or compromised his ethics in some way. I had listened to an elder's confession of immorality, and I had seen another minister use contributed funds for his own gain.

As a result, I came to Focus on the Family during its infancy with a heavy dose of skepticism running through my veins. I was certain it wouldn't take long for me to discover Dobson's double standards. But many years have gone by, and I can agree with Paul Nelson's metaphorical examination of the man. James Dobson is simply who he says he is. He has his flaws and short-comings, of course, but I can testify that the public person is no different than the private one.

Although Dr. Dobson finally put his blessings on my efforts to publish this book, it was not without reservations and conditions. Basically, he was concerned that this manuscript would attempt to make him larger than life itself. He was well aware of the dangers of placing Christian leaders on pedestals (a subject for a subsequent chapter). He was also concerned that this volume might be premature. "It's a little like a coach bragging at half time about how he won the game," Dobson once told me. "I could still fall on my face in the fourth quarter."

Certainly that would be a valid concern if this book were nothing more than a biography. Instead, its purpose is to explore the beliefs that form a foundation for the man. In my close association with Dobson for the past eight years, I have heard him express philosophies and convictions that are not contained in any of his writings. More significantly, I have seen him put those principles into practice, and I have witnessed their effectiveness.

The following pages will not only convey the story of James Dobson's life to this point but will also assess what makes him tick. This book, then, is an attempt to tell "the rest of the story." It will examine Dr. Dobson's life as though it were a piece of fabric woven with various fibers of family heritage, religious convictions, and personal values. The ensuing chapters will pull that fabric apart and examine these fibers one by one. They will also draw on his unpublished writings and give him an opportunity to respond to his critics. We will even hear from Shirley.

It is important to state again that the theme of this manuscript is not James Dobson but the biblical principles by which he has strived to live his life. Ultimately, if this book is to be worthwhile, it will be so because the reader has been pointed beyond James Dobson to the God whom he serves.

2

His Father's Son

The human mind is beautifully designed to protect itself from memories that are painful or threatening. It works by simply "forgetting" early unpleasant experiences, even though they remain recorded somewhere in the unconscious reservoir. A person's earliest recollections, then, reveal a great deal about the quality of life during the youngest years. For example, people who were abused or rejected as children are often unable to recall much prior to eight or ten years of age. Their minds have sealed off the details to prevent severe pain from oozing into the conscious mind. Others who were more secure are granted access to the earliest memories, which typically focus on warm and happy experiences.

Following this theory, James Dobson must have had a secure and loving childhood. His earliest recollection of his mother is from his infancy, perhaps around one year old. He was in her arms and she was feeding him Pablum. He can still recall the smell of that cereal-like food and that another woman (unidentified) was in the room with them. A panorama of other pleasant memories of his mother still exists from the second birthday forward.

Equally indicative of a secure beginning is Dobson's first memory of his father. He estimates himself to have been thirty months old at the time. He was at home with his mother when

11

they heard a knock on the front door. Jimmy ran to see who was there. Standing on the steps was his lanky, 6'4" father, and he was smiling.

"Hurry! Hurry! Come with me," he said excitedly to his son.

Jimmy ran to catch up with his dad as they rounded the corner of the house. There in the shadows sat a brand-new tricycle. It was big, it was blue, and it was beautiful. How interesting that the thrill of that moment survives in Dobson's mind more than fifty years later and provides a beginning point for his great love for his father. What followed was a lifelong friendship that grew richer and deeper with the passage of time.

This unusually close relationship was noted in two cover stories published in *Christianity Today*. Both pieces, written by different authors six years apart (1982 and 1988), came to the same conclusion and carried an identical title, "His Father's Son." (Incidentally, the artist who prepared the cover of the 1988 article hand-tinted an early black and white photo of Jim, Jr. and his father. He gave them both bright red hair. In truth, they were both blond before turning somewhat gray.)

Jim, Jr. has written and spoken often about his father and the enormous influence this man had on his intellectual and spiritual development. Those who have heard or read these accounts have tended to fall into one of two broad classifications. Either they also had warm and nurturing relationships with their dads and identified thoroughly with the stories and emotions shared by Dobson, or else they had unloving fathers and have spent a lifetime searching for what was missing in their lives. Either way, they were drawn to this psychologist who described so beautifully the way it *ought* to be. As such, he provided a role model for many men who had no proper masculine perspective of parenting. The third film in the original *Focus on the Family* film series, entitled "Christian Fathering," centers on the role of the dad. According to the publisher, it has now been seen by an estimated sixty million people worldwide. We can only suppose how many homes are different—and better—because of the influence of this graphic illustration.

The legacy of Rev. James Clayton Dobson, Sr. continues to the present day. A visit to his son's office at the Focus on the Family headquarters reveals the affectionate relationship these two men shared. Hanging on the walls are original oil paintings signed with a familiar name. (Dobson's father often said with a twinkle in his eye, "Don't forget that I had the name first!") Scattered in strategic places are the elder Dobson's works of sculpture. The books he owned are evident in the library. There, in prominent places, are sophisticated texts on art, astronomy, physics, anthropology, history, and religion. Finally, in a place of honor by the door is a pencil drawing of Dobson's father, looking down pensively. It captures the soul of the man. It was drawn by his most talented art student, Ray Craighead, a few months before Dobson's death. Clearly, one cannot walk through the halls of Focus on the Family without knowing that a much-loved man, now gone, has inspired the service being rendered there.

But who was this quiet, sensitive man who has been so honored and loved by his son? Dobson's book *Straight Talk to Men and Their Wives* tells the story in part, but the root of it is found in his father's childhood. James Dobson, Sr. was born on May 24, 1911, as the youngest son in a house full of boys, who were later joined by a baby sister. Almost from infancy he was seen to have a classic "artistic" temperament. At three years of age, he announced that he wanted to be a great painter. Other boys hoped to become firemen and policemen, but "Jimmie" was steadfast. Throughout his elementary and high school years, his career objective remained constant. Art was his passion, and he apparently had the talent to reach his cherished goals.

One pivotal day during his sixteenth year, he heard an inner voice as he walked along the street toward home. It was inaudible to the human ear, but it was real. It said, "I want you to set aside your great ambition to be an artist and prepare for a life of service in the ministry!" He recognized the inaudible voice of God, and it terrified him.

"No! No, Lord!" he replied. "You know I have my plans all made and that art is my one consuming interest." But the impulse to preach continued unchecked. He said later that he would argue with God and try to suppress the matter, but it always returned more forcefully than before. That war between his will and the will of God went on for more than two years.

Finally, as he got out of bed one morning during his senior year of high school, he heard the voice again. It said, "Today, you will have to make up your mind." He wrestled with the issue all that day at school, but told no one. He came home that afternoon to find the house empty. He paced back and forth in the living room, crying and praying and struggling with this unrelenting demand of God. Finally in an act of defiance, he suddenly turned his face upward and said, "It's too great a price and I won't pay it!"

He later described that moment as the most terrible experience of his life. The presence of God seemed to leave him as one person would walk away from another. You may interpret this event from your own theological perspective, of course, but Jimmie Dobson later described what he knew to have occurred. Art had become his god. It mattered more to him than anything on earth, and indeed, he chose to sacrifice his faith rather than give it up. God will not tolerate *anything* that competes with His preeminence in our lives, and it is not uncommon for Him to test us at the point of our disobedience. Dobson failed the test. Seven long years would pass before he would hear that still, small voice again.

James Dobson, Sr.'s father was a successful businessman by that time, being co-owner of a Coca-Cola plant with the first man to put the drink in a bottle. This allowed him to send all of his children through college. He asked his youngest son to pick out any school in the country to attend, and Jimmie chose the Art Institute of Pittsburgh. In the fall of 1930 he enrolled and embarked upon the career he had coveted from his earliest childhood. It soon became obvious that he had the ability to succeed in the world of art. On graduation day the Institute ranked the students according to talent, and Jimmie Dobson was called to the front of the auditorium to receive the highest rating in his class. As he walked that long aisle to receive the symbolic "Number One" on his paintings, he remembered a Scripture he had learned as a child. It said, "Except the Lord build the house, they labor in vain that build it" (Ps. 127:1).

Still deeply in rebellion against God, Jimmie Dobson set out on his journey to the top of the art world. Unfortunately, the Great Depression had paralyzed America by that time, and he couldn't find a job of any type. He walked the streets in desperation and eventually took a job pumping gas at a Texaco service station. There, in that frustrating circumstance, with his dreams slowly ebbing away, the Lord forced him to confront his carnal ambition and selfish desires. He later referred to those days as his "Egyptian Bondage."

For those who believe in the power of prayer, and even those who do not, *stay tuned!* Right at the moment of despair, the president of the Art Institute of Pittsburgh, Mr. Willard Shook, wrote Dobson a letter. He offered him a position as an instructor at an unheard-of salary of three hundred dollars per month. But that letter was lost before it could be mailed. A year later, after Dobson had accepted the call to preach and reestablished his relationship with Jesus Christ, Mr. Shook found the old letter on his desk and sent it, along with a new letter, saying, "I wondered why you never even did me the courtesy of replying to my offer."

Why did Jimmie Dobson fail to receive that first letter? Because his ninety-seven-pound mother was praying for his soul every day of her life. She was pleading with the Lord to bring her youngest son back into the fold. If he had received Mr. Shook's original letter, his life would have turned in the direction of art. That would have advantageous for others in a similar situation, but for the senior Dobson it would have meant continued rebellion against God. Certainly it would have changed the world into which his only son was born two years later and would have had far-reaching consequences for the future. Everything hinged on the delivery of a single piece of mail.

About the same time, Jimmie met and fell madly in love with a preacher's pretty daughter named Myrtle Georgia Dillingham. She also was in a state of spiritual rebellion, and they made a perfect match. She had vowed she would never marry a minister, and indeed, she didn't. She was wed on June 13, 1934, to a temporarily sidetracked artist whose ambition still burned within his breast. They both knew he would make it to the top—someday!

Then something dramatic occurred that was to turn their world upside down. Every day of the Dobsons' lives from that point on was to be rearranged by what seemed like a chance encounter in the fall of 1934. Their son described it this way in his book *Parenting Isn't for Cowards:*

My grandmother had prayed for her six children throughout their formative years, but her youngest son (my father) was a particularly

15

headstrong young man. For seven years following his high school graduation, he had left the church and rejected its teachings. Then, as it happened, an evangelist came to town, and a great spiritual awakening swept their local church. But my father would have no part of it and refused even to attend.

One evening as the rest of the family was preparing to go to church, my father (who was visiting his parents' home) slipped away and hid on the side porch. He could hear his brothers chatting as they boarded the car. Then one of them, Willis, said suddenly, "Hey, where's Jim? Isn't he going tonight?"

Someone else said, "No, Willis. He said he isn't ever going to church again."

My father heard his brother get out of the car and begin searching for him all over the house. Willis had experienced a personal relationship with Jesus Christ when he was nine years old, and he loved the Lord passionately. He had held tightly to his faith throughout adolescence when his brothers (including my father) mocked him unmercifully. They had called him "Preacher Boy," "Sissy" and "Goody-Goody." It only made him more determined to do what was right.

My dad remained silent as Willis hurried throughout the house calling his name. Finally, he found his brother sitting silently in the swing on the side porch.

"Jim," he said, "aren't you going with us to the service tonight?"

My dad said, "No, Willis. I'm through with all of that. I don't plan to ever go back again."

Willis said nothing. But as my father sat looking at the floor, he saw big tears splashing on his brother's shoes. My father was deeply moved that Willis would love him that much, after the abuse he had taken for his Christian stand.

"I'll go just because it means that much to him," my dad said to himself.

Because of the delay my father had caused, the family was late arriving at the church that night. The only seats left were on the second row from the front. They streamed down the aisle and were seated. A song evangelist was singing and the words began to speak to my dad's heart.

Just that quickly, he yielded. After seven years of rebellion and sin, it was over. He was forgiven. He was clean.

The evangelist at that time was a man named Bona Fleming, who was unusually anointed of God. When the singer concluded, Reverend Fleming walked across the platform and put his foot on the altar rail. He leaned forward and pointed his finger directly at my dad.

"You! Young man! Right there! Stand up!"

My father rose to his feet.

"Now, I want you to tell all these people what God did for you while the singer was singing!"

My dad gave his first testimony, through his tears, of the forgiveness and salvation he had just received. Willis was crying too. So was my grandmother. She had prayed for him unceasingly for more than seven years.

What had happened during the song that had such a dramatic effect on Jimmie Dobson? It should not be difficult to guess. He had heard that inner voice again. It said, "Son, are we going to do business again?"

He said, "Yes, Lord. I want nothing but Your will in my life."

"Then let's go back to the living room where we left off seven years ago."

"Do you mean the call to preach?" he asked.

"That's exactly what I mean," said the Lord.

"All right. I will obey," was his reply.

For all practical purposes, Dobson laid aside his passion for art that night. He never expected to pursue it again. This talent that God had given him as a lad no longer stood between him and his Maker. But once he surrendered, God graciously gave the gift back to him, and he used it for the rest of his life in service to the kingdom.

A few days later, the two letters from Willard Shook arrived, offering the kind of position for which Dobson had longed. But now he replied, "No, thanks," and explained that he was going into the ministry. His life had taken a new turn. Shortly thereafter, Myrtle also knelt at an altar of prayer and accepted God's will in her life, even if it meant being married to a poor, despised preacher of the gospel. She stood by his side for forty-three more years!

"Humble" best describes their unsteady beginnings in the ministry. With the depression still raging, it was difficult to keep bread on the table. Furthermore, the only child they were able to bear was born on April 21, 1936, which added to the financial strain. As for the new dad, he had missed his chance to go to seminary and was now struggling through a correspondence course to qualify for a local preacher's license. Finally, when that

17

requirement was met, he approached the District Superintendent in the Church of the Nazarene and asked if there was a little church somewhere that he might lead. In response, he was invited to preach a "trial sermon" for a congregation that had recently lost its minister. Years later he wrote of that painful experience and thereby provided us with a valuable window into his heart.

Woven throughout the account are the fibers of his character—his vulnerability, his kindness, his sensitivity, and his generosity. These admirable traits were his hallmarks and have become characteristic of his son as well. This is what he wrote:

I settled myself comfortably that Saturday morning in the familiar seat in the chair-car. It was purely incidental that Mena, Arkansas, my destination, was on the Kansas City Southern, the railroad that my father had served as a conductor for so long. The presiding elder of our denomination had met with the official board of the church, which was without a pastor, and they had agreed to allow me to come and preach for them in the two Sunday services.

This was the first and last time that I was ever to submit myself to the indignity of a "trial sermon." But I was totally ignorant of the ways of the ministry, and too, I was hardly in a favorable bargaining position. I thought back over the events of the past week.

Since I had given up my job as manager of a Texaco service station, I had worked very hard to prepare myself for getting a local preacher's license. I had finished the home study course, as required, in record time, working through the hot summer months, ten or twelve hours a day, all the while enduring the silent disapproval of my brothers. If I could get a small church to pastor, it was my intention to finish college and get the experience necessary to be ordained. Since I already had the equivalent of three years of college training, I thought that this would not be very difficult to do.

I was tense. Myrtle, my wife, had left our four-and-a-half month old son in the care of my mother. We had earnestly prayed as she drove to the station, asking God's help if Mena was indeed to be the place for us. We reminded Him that I was stepping out by faith into a new field, about which I knew nothing.

My "call to preach" was a very real thing to me, but I recalled a sermon that I had recently heard. "A call to preach is *not* a guarantee of success, but only the guarantee of the possibility of success." One had to use all the industry, sense and sacrifice too, that he could muster. I was ready to give it my best. Myrtle kissed me warmly. There were

18

tears in her eyes. Having been brought up in a minister's home she knew far better than I the trials and sacrifices that a pastor must endure, especially in a small church.

"I'll be praying for you, honey," her voice came back to me as I stepped onto the train.

The journey took a good part of the day, and you may be sure I went over my two sermons meticulously. On arrival, I went immediately to a small hotel and registered. After eating a bite, I walked around the town. It was not unfamiliar to me. In fact, my mother and father had once lived there (before I was born), and I had visited the place many times. I walked by the church and looked it over. It was a white frame building on a nice corner lot. Having surveyed the scene, I returned to my hotel room and retired early.

An eternity later, Sunday morning and the time for the service arrived. Of course, I would go to Sunday School. I took my Bible and went walking toward the church. When I got a block away, I saw another man who looked strikingly like a preacher, with a Bible under his arm, approaching the church from the opposite direction. We met on the church steps and I introduced myself.

"I am James Dobson. District Superintendent, Dr. Brian, sent me to preach two trial sermons here today."

He looked at me in surprise and said, "There must be some mistake. I am Ben Harley, and Dr. Brian distinctly told me to come here and preach two trial sermons today."

I was totally and utterly dismayed and confused by his statement. What was the ethical thing to do in a case like this? Rev. Harley was an older man with many years of experience. I did the only thing there was to be done, which was to bow out of the picture gracefully.

"Since there was a mistake," I said, "you go ahead and preach. I will simply sit back and enjoy the services." (What I was thinking of that District Superintendent about then should not be published!)

But Rev. Harley would not hear to my suggestion. He proposed a better solution. "Why not let me take one service and you take the other?" On his insistence, I agreed. I knew the odds were all against me. He was already in a pastorate not many miles away and was simply desiring a change. I was looking for my first charge. He had twenty-five years of experience, while I was a rank beginner. I would be preaching my third sermon, which I knew would be in the most difficult of circumstances, while my experienced rival would calmly sit back and survey my struggle. There was another element too that caused me some concern: The Superintendent had not been too friendly. I thought I detected that he did not want me in his district. Nevertheless, I swallowed my pride and went through with it.

Rev. Harley's Sunday morning message was filled with denominational cliches and bombast. He was obviously preaching one of his "sugar stick" sermons that he had often used before. The congregation, however, was very receptive.

After the service I went home to dinner with the town banker. I learned later that he was a member of the official board. We had a courteous conversation in which he asked me a lot of the usual questions—about myself, whether I was married, how many children I had, and what preparation I had for the ministry.

Time for the night service came. The reader will forgive me I am sure if I draw the curtain over my miserable efforts to preach that night. Ministers have a term for it. It's called "getting in the brush."

My text was a good one—Hebrews 11:13. The main thought of my sermon was to show the Christian as a stranger in an alien world, who is sustained by his faith in the promises of God. He works and patiently endures deprivation and want, if necessary, in order to receive an entrance into that city "which hath foundations, whose builder and maker is God."

It is certain that the sermon had one application. *I* was a stranger and a pilgrim in this place and, from all indications, about to move on shortly. I was going to need "soothing and sustaining" from somewhere when it was over!

The board met immediately, and it took them only a little while to make their decision. Their spokesman came to me first. He was "so sorry" to tell me that they had called the other man. There was nothing against me, I was given to understand. I was a fine young man. He was sure I would find a good church somewhere, etc. He gave me an envelope which he said contained some "expense money." He regretted that I had come so far—at least this is the substance of what he told me. I thanked him and shook hands with Rev. Harley and hoped that he would have a great ministry in Mena.

When I got to the hotel, I opened the envelope. It contained three dollars! I'll admit I brushed a few tears from my eyes as I packed my suitcase to catch the night train home.

I was sitting there on the train thinking it all over, when a poor woman came down the aisle. She was dressed in cheap ragged clothes and was trying to handle several small children. They took the seat opposite me. Presently, I heard the conductor ask for her ticket. She began to cry. She had no ticket, she said, but she was just going to see her mother who was at death's door. It was only a few miles down the road to her destination. "Please don't put us off the train," she pleaded. "I promise to pay the railroad back when I get some money."

Before the conductor could reply, I took the three dollars out of my pocket and paid her fare. I felt a great sense of oneness with all the little people and all the frustrated people in the world that night!

It was not easy to tell Myrtle of my misfortunes; but once I had come out with it, we began to laugh at the comic aspects of the situation. She was understanding, but now we began to get in earnest with our praying. Those were the first of more dark days to come!

In a few days, we were appointed to a church in New Orleans. Although we wanted a pastorate so badly, I could not feel right about this appointment. The nearer the time came to go, the more both of us felt that it was out of divine order somehow. At length, we went to the station to buy my ticket, when, to my surprise the agent told me that the train schedule had been changed and that the one I was supposed to catch had already left the station. He said there was a bad labor strike underway and advised me that I might be better off having missed it.

When I turned to tell Myrtle, I felt so relieved. An inner voice seemed to assure me that it was all right, that I ought not to go. The next morning I read in the paper that, indeed, that train had been fired upon by strikers and, in fact, had never reached its destination.

Myrtle said, "James, God has more than one way to lead people. He leads them by closing doors as well as by opening them."

But we prayed out of desperation now. We had spent most of our morning on our knees. It was just about noon when we began to strike a victorious note. It was all right. God had not forgotten us! The answer was on its way! This was the feeling I had, and I took my young wife in my arms and we wept and rejoiced together.

At that precise moment, a telegram was delivered to the door. With trembling hands I tore it open and read:

Am appointing you pastor of the Church in Sulphur Springs, Texas. Can you be there for the first services, November 22? Would like to see you personally before you go. Signed, Jarrell Aycock, District Superintendent, Dallas District.

I might add that I had met Dr. Aycock only a short time before; I had explained my situation to him. The following recommendation reflects the lack of confidence that I had in my own ministry at that time.

"You have heard of practicing physicians," I said. "Well, I am a practicing preacher! If you have a little church somewhere that is so

21

run-down at the heels, so poor and so sorry that you are sure I can't hurt it, then that's where I want to be a pastor. Don't give me a good church because I'm afraid I will tear it up."

When I got to Sulphur Springs, I was sorry I had been so specific.

His first pastorate was indeed difficult. Located in the northeastern corner of Texas, the church had only ten members and a budget of two dollars per week. The community of Sulphur Springs (Dobson sometimes called it "Suffering Springs") was locked in the grip of poverty. It is difficult in these affluent days to recall the utter squalor and despair of small Texas towns during the depression, but the residents from that era certainly remember. Mere survival was a triumph. Rev. and Mrs. Dobson moved into that environment and began reaching out to the humble people. By the time they left five years later to enter the evangelistic field, their church had 250 members—quite large for such a small community. They were greatly loved by the people.

Those who knew Rev. Dobson during that period described him as "a good, decent man." He journeyed from farm to farm in search of anyone wanting to know Jesus. One of the members of the church in Sulphur Springs was a seventeen-year-old boy named Noble Hathaway. Noble stuttered so badly he could hardly be understood, but he grew spiritually under Rev. Dobson's ministry.

Then God did a curious thing. He called Noble to the ministry. There has never been a less likely candidate for Christian leadership. Yet with the encouragement of Jimmie and Myrtle Dobson, he went to college, was healed of the worst of his stuttering, and became a productive minister of the gospel. Indeed, he and his wife, Gwendolyn, became fast friends of the Dobsons and served together in the cause of Christ for many years.

Noble is the sole survivor of that foursome today. If you ask him about the contribution Jimmie and Myrtle Dobson made to his life, he is likely to cry. "They loved me when I was unlovable," he will say. "You also need to know that Jimmie Dobson was, above all else, a man of prayer."

Dr. Leslie Parrott, who is now the president of Olivet Nazarene University in Kankakee, Illinois, also remembered Rev. Dobson as a prayer warrior. "I first met the Dobsons in the 1940s when they came to conduct a series of meetings at a church I pastored. We had one of the outstanding revivals of my lifetime during that week. The church was filled to capacity every night, and we had marvelous spiritual results.

"Jim and Myrtle stayed in our little parsonage. We lived in the front bedroom and gave them the back bedroom. Only a small bathroom separated us, and in that close proximity for several days, we got to know the Dobsons quite well. Jim had one habit that was new to me. Every morning he rose at four o'clock and began to pray. He didn't pray like the Lord was near; he really poured it on! It wasn't long before the rest of us woke up and decided that we might as well join him."

It was Rev. Dobson's practice to spend three to four hours each day in prayer when he was conducting meetings. That was the only way he felt adequate to the task. He often took long walks with his little dog, while he communed with the Lord. Prayer was his life. And God honored that commitment by blessing his speaking ministry with wonderful results. Many people came to know the Savior after hearing his presentation of the gospel message. Before long the young preacher became the prominent evangelist in the Church of the Nazarene, being booked for four years in advance. He was a man on a mission and was so absorbed in his work that he was rarely distracted from it.

On one occasion, when he was preaching in a tent erected in a small town, he became so engrossed in his message that he failed to notice a big cat sleeping on the platform. James, Sr. was not an animated speaker, but he often walked around as he spoke. In the midst of his sermon, he stepped on the tail of the cat and just stood on it. Those were the days during World War II when car brakes squeaked loudly, and Dobson later explained that he thought the cat's screeching was just an automobile coming to a stop at the corner. So he continued to stand on the cat's tail, while the poor feline screamed in pain and desperately clawed at the carpet to escape the weight of this 180-pound man. To overcome the distraction, Rev. Dobson simply raised his voice and continued preaching the word that God had laid on his heart!

Although he was a serious man who considered his calling with utmost sincerity, James, Sr. was not above laughing at himself. One of his favorite stories described an incident at a tiny country church where he was scheduled to preach. A few minutes before the evening service, he decided to use the restroom, which was located on the front side of the building. People were gathering for the services, so he pressed past them and entered the small room. When he was ready to exit, he turned the doorknob and discovered it wouldn't work. No matter how hard he tried to open it, the lock would not budge. Then he forgot which direction was locked and which unlocked. James, Sr. suffered from mild claustrophobia, and the knowledge that he was closeted against his will caused him to panic. He tried taking a deep breath, but the walls were closing in on him. In desperation, he backed to one wall and threw his full weight against the door. It burst open with a crack as the door frame splintered, and he came rolling out head over heels on the grassy lawn. When he looked up, the people to whom he was about to preach were looking down at him in wonder. He spoke that evening with large grass stains on both knees of his pants. On nights like that, his strong sense of God's calling must have been the only thing that pulled him through!

Years later, an article in *Christianity Today* summarized him in this way: "A man more unlike the stereotype of a traveling evangelist would be hard to imagine. He was a quiet, vulnerable, deeply compassionate man. Nazarenes were a fervent people, but he was not particularly demonstrative. He showed no interest *in* or talent *for* promoting himself, though his deep sincerity penetrated people."

His father's love for Jesus Christ did not escape the notice of Jim, Jr. At one year of age, he attempted to pray with his parents before he learned to talk. He would imitate the sounds they were making as they communicated with God.

And just as his father had, young Jim made a dramatic decision when he was three years old that would shape the rest of his life. A half century later, he wrote about that vivid moment:

I remember the occasion clearly today. I was attending a Sunday evening church service and was sitting near the back with my mother. My father was the pastor, and he invited those who wished to do so to come pray at the altar. Fifteen or twenty people went forward, and I joined them spontaneously. I recall crying and asking Jesus to forgive my sins. I know that sounds strange, but that's the way it occurred. It is overwhelming for me to think about that event today. Imagine the King of the universe, Creator of all heaven and earth, caring about an insignificant kid barely out of toddlerhood! It makes no sense, but I know it happened.

The decision to accept Jesus as Lord is the most important event in any person's life. The Bible reports that the angels literally rejoice every time someone decides to join the family of God. But the Dobson family held a special celebration over Jim's decision because it was the fulfillment of a prophecy given by his maternal great-grandfather, George McCluskey. This patriarch of the family was also a man of prayer who spent hours every day petitioning God specifically for the spiritual welfare of his offspring.

During one intimate moment in prayer, McCluskey received an assurance that every member of his family for four successive generations (including his own) would serve Jesus as Lord. That promise moved one step closer to reality when Jim knelt at an altar of prayer.

With the passage of time a deep friendship and bond developed between Jim and his father. Because Rev. Dobson traveled a lot, he sought ways to compensate his young son for time spent on the road. He made a deliberate effort to spend long hours with his son during the interludes at home. Those were special days for the two of them as they hunted, fished, and played tennis together. But the moments they shared were not spent on recreation alone. James, Sr. used the quiet mornings in the woods to talk to his son about his love of learning and about spiritual matters.

Dobson now recalls those days as among the happiest of his life:

My dad and I would arise before the sun came up on a wintry morning. We would put on our hunting clothes and heavy boots and drive twenty miles from the little town where we lived. After parking the car and climbing over a fence, we would enter a wooded area, which I called the "big woods" because the trees seemed so large to me. We would slip down to the creek bed and follow that winding stream several miles back into the forest.

Then my dad would hide me under a fallen tree, which made a

little room with its branches. He would find a similar shelter for himself around a bend in the creek. Then we would await the arrival of the sun and the awakening of the animal world. Little squirrels and birds and chipmunks would scurry back and forth, not knowing they were being observed. My dad and I then watched as the breathtaking panorama of the morning unfolded, which spoke so eloquently of the God who made all things.

But most importantly, there was something dramatic that occurred between my dad and me out there in the forest. An intense love and affection was generated on those mornings that set the tone for a lifetime of fellowship. There was a closeness and a oneness that made me want to be like that man . . . that made me choose his values as my values, his dreams as my dreams, his God as my God.

Years later, when James, Jr. had become Dr. Dobson, the counselor to millions, he still leaned heavily on the advice of his father, who was by then a professor of art and history at a liberal arts college in Olathe, Kansas. The elder Dobson was an avid reader who was fascinated with medicine, biochemistry, astronomy, sociology, theology, and music, as well as many other areas. He became a fountain of information and a trusted researcher for his son's projects. He often sent relevant articles, clippings, and books to his son, along with his own observations and beliefs.

Working closely with Dr. Dobson, I have observed how he has inherited his father's immeasurable curiosity for life. But more importantly, he has a hunger to know more about the Creator whose footprints he sees all around him. Once, when we were at the airport checking in for a flight, I offered to hold his briefcase since he had several pieces of luggage. In the bustle of the moment, he apparently didn't hear me. A few minutes later I wandered off to buy a newspaper, taking the briefcase with me. Suddenly, one of my associates came running down the hallway and said, "Dr. Dobson lost his briefcase, and he's frantically looking for it because his research Bible is inside."

When I joined Dr. Dobson, he opened the briefcase and pulled out a tattered Bible. "I wouldn't take $1,000 for this Bible," he said as he lovingly thumbed through it. On every page he had underlined passages and written extensive notes in the margins. I doubt that many preachers have a study Bible with more personal commentary than James Dobson's!

James, Sr.'s lifetime of accumulating such knowledge proved to be an invaluable resource for his son. In fact, he served in an editorial capacity for the psychologist's writings. Prior to publication, Jim would bring his manuscripts to his father for review. The two of them would sit for lengthy periods in silence while the elder Dobson carefully read his son's writings. Occasionally, he would lift his head and contemplate some aspect of the manuscript and then quietly begin reading again. Finally, the silence would be broken, and he would begin sharing his thoughts and reactions while Jim took notes. That is the kind of relationship they had.

They were partners in every sense of the word, but in the fall of 1977 they received an ominous foreshadowing that their special friendship was about to end. Dr. Dobson was speaking in San Antonio to the Texas Pediatric Society when an urgent telephone message came from Dr. Paul Cunningham, his father's pastor.

"Your dad is dying," Paul said. "He has had a heart attack and is now developing both arrhythmia and congestion. That is usually a fatal combination following a myocardial infarction. We don't expect him to live through the night. Come as quickly as you can get here!"

Dr. and Mrs. Dobson boarded a plane and headed for Kansas City. The trip lasted less than three hours, but it seemed forever as they contemplated the loss of his father. When they arrived at the airport, they were met by a longtime friend, who was smiling.

"Your dad is remarkably better," she said. "In fact, he's waiting to see you at the hospital."

They spent several hours chatting and reminiscing about their days together. In his book *Straight Talk to Men and Their Wives*, Dr. Dobson wrote about his visit:

I will always be thankful for having the priceless opportunity to see him alive, again—to express those words of appreciation and love that we seldom convey before it is too late. I stood by his bed in that intensive care unit. There amidst beeping oscilloscopes and bottles of glucose, I patted those delicate artistic hands that I have loved since my earliest awareness. He was entirely calm and coherent, revealing no hint of his brush with death.

27

Approximately two months later, on December 4, 1977, God summoned his servant home. It was a Sunday afternoon, and Rev. Dobson had just prayed for dinner. Suddenly, he was seized by another heart attack that proved fatal. He fell into the arms of his beloved wife and was gone. Paramedics arrived shortly thereafter, but they were unable to revive him.

The news of his father's passing was devastating to Jim, Jr. Although he knew he would see him again on the other side, the gulf of separation seemed so wide at the moment. Gone were the long telephone conversations, the joyful holiday visits, and the warm letters that had given them so many happy moments. Gone, too, were the prayers, the humorous stories, and the theories they had shared. Gone was his father, his advisor, his editor, and his friend.

At the memorial service two days later, Jim steadied himself long enough to deliver a eulogy that conveyed his personal sense of loss. In this tribute he described the love he had felt from his father:

I'm told that when I was a small child, perhaps three years of age, we lived in a one-bedroom apartment. My little bed was located beside the bed of my parents. Dad said it was not uncommon during that time for him to awaken at night and hear a little voice whispering, "Daddy? Daddy?"

He would answer quietly, "What, Jimmy?"

Then I would reply, "Hold my hand!"

My dad would reach across the darkness and grope for my little hand, finally engulfing it in his. He said the instant he encompassed my hand, my arm would become limp and my breathing deep and regular. I had gone back to sleep. You see, I only wanted to know that he was *there!* I have been reaching for him throughout my forty-one years, and he has always been there. And now for the first time in my life, he's gone.

So where do we go from here? Do we leave this church today in despair and discouragement? Certainly not, although our sorrow is incalculable. But my dad is not in that casket before us. He is *alive*, and we will soon see him again. He has achieved the pearl of eternal life, which is our heritage, too. Life will soon be over for everyone in this sanctuary—and for everyone whom we love. Therefore, I have determined to live each day as Christ would dictate, keeping in mind the temporal nature of everything which now seems so permanent. Even in death, you see, my dad has taught me about life.

Thank you for allowing me to share my deepest feelings and emotions today. I must acknowledge, in closing, that James Dobson was not a perfect man. It would be unfortunate to eulogize him in a way that would embarrass him if he were sitting among us. My father had a generous assortment of flaws, even as you and I. But I loved him. Perhaps as much as any son ever loved his dad.

Danae and Ryan, you had a great man for a grandfather. Not because he was president or because he will be remembered in the history books. He was great because of his uncompromising dedication to the Christian faith. And if I can be half the father to you that he was to me, you will be fortunate children, indeed.

James Dobson, Sr. was buried December 7, 1977, in Olathe, Kansas, on a wind-swept hill where he had often walked with his little dog, Benji. On his tombstone are inscribed two simple words that summarize his life better than any benediction: "He prayed."

A FINAL NOTE

Six years after the death of James Dobson, Sr., his son received the following letter from a man named Jim Lepper, whom he had never met.

Dear Dr. Dobson:

I am a firefighter on the Kansas City, Missouri, Fire Department. In my fifteen-year career some incidents stand out by themselves. One such call affected me differently. Your father had collapsed moments before we received the call. I think this particular day may have been a holiday or a Sunday. When the call came in, I drove the apparatus to the scene, and with me were two men, my captain and a firefighter. When we arrived, the other two men ran in and started CPR. I put the block down under a wheel and entered the house. It seems like five or six people were in the house. The table was nicely set with silver and china. My captain and the firefighter were starting to work on the man who was lying on the floor. My job, then, was to gather information from a relative concerning name, age, phone number, and medication. I also saw it as part of my duty to help in giving comfort to the people in need. As many times before, the lady who identified herself as the patient's wife was unable to give me the information. She started to ask me of the welfare of her husband. The ambulance crew arrived while we were talking. Usually, we tell the relatives that we are trying to stabilize the patient for transfer and dodge the question, unless we are guessing that the patient is doing o.k., in which case we try to help people see the bright side of the situation.

Your mother asked me if your father was going to be all right. Not knowing the background of your parents, I took a chance that could have gotten me in a lot of trouble with my superiors (I have never answered like this before or since). I told her that if he knew Jesus, he was o.k. She responded that he was a Nazarene minister. The question was still on her face, and I answered her again that if he knew Jesus he was o.k. She told me that he had been an art professor for eight years at the Nazarene college. I responded the same as before, and again she spoke in a way that would cause a person to think he was not only a Christian, but an important leader in the church. She had been holding back the tears. I looked her straight in the eyes and softly said, "If he knows Jesus, he is all right." The tears were held back no longer as she finally realized that he had probably died. She said, "He knows Jesus; he's all right." I think she felt some peace at that time, knowing that if he was no longer alive in the flesh, he was with his Lord.

I thought you might want to hear this version of what happened on the day your father passed on. In hearing you speak of him, I would rather have known him in his life instead of showing up at his death.

My own father is not a Christian yet. Please pray for his salvation.

Your brother in Christ,

Jim Lepper

3

A Mother's Love

James Dobson, Sr. and Myrtle Georgia Dillingham were virtually penniless when they married in 1934. It seemed that everybody was poor those days, except the likes of John D. Rockefeller and Henry Ford. The Great Depression held the world in its vicelike grip and forced many young families to postpone their dreams and ambitions. It certainly paralyzed the Dobsons. They couldn't even afford to live together at first. For three months they kept their marriage a secret in order to continue living for free in each of their parents' homes.

There was no shortage of love in their relationship, however. Both Jimmie and Myrtle came from families where divorce was unheard of, and they entered into marriage as a lifelong contract. In fact, Jimmie expressed the depths of his commitment to Myrtle a few months before their secret wedding. A copy of that statement survives today. It was given to Jim, Jr. some forty years later, written on a crumpled sheet of paper. Note Rev. Dobson's reference to Christian values, even though he was in a state of spiritual rebellion at the time:

I want you to understand and be fully aware of my feelings concerning the marriage covenant which we are about to enter. I have been taught at my mother's knee, and in harmony with the Word of God, that the marriage vows are inviolable, and by entering into them I am binding myself absolutely and for life. The idea of estrangement from you through divorce for any reason at all (although God allows

31

one—infidelity) will never at any time be permitted to enter into my thinking. I'm not naive in this. On the contrary, I'm fully aware of the possibility, unlikely as it now appears, that mutual incompatibility or other unforeseen circumstances could result in extreme mental suffering. If such becomes the case, I am resolved for my part to accept it as a consequence of the commitment I am now making, and to bear it if necessary, to the end of our lives together.

I have loved you dearly as a sweetheart and will continue to love you as my wife. But over and above that, I love you with a Christian love that demands that I never react in any way toward you that would jeopardize our prospects of entering heaven, which is the supreme objective of both our lives. And I pray that God Himself will make our affection for one another perfect and eternal.

How could a young man only twenty-three years of age make such a mature pledge? How could he make a lifetime commitment with so much certainty? Obviously, these words would amount to an empty promise if he were relying on his own wisdom and hopes. (A 50 percent divorce rate today proves the fallibility of man's best intentions.) The answer lies in the fact that he was basing his marriage relationship on the principles authored by God Himself. These precepts had been tested and found true for thousands of years. The marriage of James and Myrtle lasted forty-three years—until death temporarily came between them. They never veered from the wedding vows exchanged in 1934, and they enjoyed all the blessings God intended for a permanent relationship between a man and woman.

Of course, this does not mean they spent every moment in perfect bliss. James and Myrtle were as different as night and day, and they struggled mightily to harmonize their diverse temperaments. While he was contemplative and introspective, she was active and outgoing. Where he was intellectual and reserved, she was practical and profoundly social. "James, Sr. enjoyed being with other people, but if given his preference, he would rather be alone painting, reading, or studying," a family member said. "Myrtle, on the other hand, loved fellowship. She never wanted to miss a single conversation. She wanted to be in on everything."

Their son also observed these characteristics. "They both

had intense personalities and saw everything differently, even though they were absolutely committed to each other," he said. "When it came to the important, overriding decisions, my mother always yielded to the leadership of my father. She had profound respect for him. Nevertheless, they could argue endlessly about such mundane things as how to pack suitcases into the trunk of a car, or which hotel to select for the night. But if an idea ever got past both of them, you knew it was good."

One of those good ideas was their son, James, Jr., whose birth in 1936 was difficult. The delivery was by Caesarean section, a risky and experimental procedure at the time.

"Any attempt to have more children could be life threatening," the physician told Myrtle. The Lord knew this in advance, of course, and He bestowed some of the best traits of each parent into this little lad who would be their sole offspring.

Being an only child also meant that young Jim was the happy recipient of his parents' total love and affection. While his father imparted principles and masculine traits to the boy, his mother modeled the virtues of the Christian family that would later become the centerpiece for his early writings.

She had no formal training in mothering, but she had an intuitive sense of how to raise her son and care for her husband. Myrtle was the embodiment of the Judeo-Christian value system that was well understood by generations of the past, but has been largely forgotten in the late twentieth century.

She knew the importance of parental leadership, of maintaining a balance between love and discipline, and of respecting the dignity and worth of every member of the family. By example, she taught Jim how realistic boundaries could be placed on a child and how they could be enforced with confident firmness. She showed him how good behavior could be molded through the use of reward and punishment.

Perhaps the best-known example of her response, when challenged, was recorded by Dr. Dobson in his book *Dare to Discipline.* In that best-selling manual for parents he wrote this account:

My own mother had an unusual understanding of good disciplinary procedures. She was very tolerant of my childishness, and I found her reasonable on most issues. If I was late coming home from school, I could just explain what had caused the delay, and that was the end of the matter. If I didn't get my work done, we could sit down and come to some kind of agreement for future action. But there was one matter on which she was absolutely rigid: She did not tolerate "sassiness."

She knew that backtalk and "lip" are the child's most potent weapons of defiance and they must be discouraged. I learned very early that if I was going to launch a flippant attack on her, I had better be standing at least ten or twelve feet away. This distance was necessary to avoid being hit with whatever she could get in her hands. On one occasion she cracked me with a shoe; at other times she used a handy belt. The day I learned the importance of staying out of reach shines like a neon light in my mind. I made the costly mistake of "sassing" her when I was about four feet away. She wheeled around to grab something with which to hit me, and her hand landed on a girdle. Now those were the days when a girdle was a weapon. It weighed about sixteen pounds and was lined with lead and steel. She drew back and swung that abominable garment in my direction, and I can still hear it whistling through the air. The intended blow caught me across the chest, followed by a multitude of straps and buckles wrapping themselves around my midsection. She gave me an entire thrashing with one massive blow! From that day forward, I cautiously retreated a few steps before popping off.

Although Jim didn't appreciate the principles behind his mother's discipline at the time, they would serve him well down the road. Years later, his mother's parenting philosophy became the model for one of his ministry themes. On the other hand, he has never recommended spankings with a sixteen-pound girdle!

When he wrote *The Strong-Willed Child*, he dedicated the book to her, saying: "She was blessed with a brilliant understanding of children. She intuitively grasped the meaning of discipline and taught me many principles which I've described on the following pages."

When Jim Dobson was a teenager, his mother's brand of justice again became apparent. By this time, his father was a full-time evangelist, and his regular travels punctuated their lives. Due to his frequent absences, Myrtle did not have the advantage of saying, "Wait until your father gets home!" (Even James Dobson was once a typical adolescent with a stubborn mind of his own.) Of course, his mother had her ways of dealing with the boy who was now taller than she was. And he gave her many opportunities to test her parenting theories.

When Jim was in the eighth grade, his English teacher assigned him to read a certain number of books during the course of the semester. Each book on an approved list was assigned a specific number of points, with the tougher and longer texts being given higher values. To achieve an A+ in the class, the student simply had to earn the required number of points by reading a sufficient number of sophisticated books.

"Hey, Mom," he said one afternoon. "You know I've been wanting to earn some extra money for the band trip that is coming up. What will you give me if I get an A+ in my reading class?"

She offered five dollars, and Jim decided to go for it. Unfortunately, he didn't go for it soon enough. He came to the end of the term and hadn't done the necessary reading. So he decided simply to cheat on the assignment. He went to the library and selected the most difficult and lengthy books on the list, including Shakespeare's writings, *Ben Hur, Aesop's Fables,* and many other classics. He then faked his reports and told the teacher he had fulfilled the required reading.

Jim's report card reflected the duplicity. He received an A+ in reading and collected the five dollars promised by his mother. Not fully realizing the wrong he had done, he admitted to her that he had beaten the system.

Myrtle reacted with alarm. "You did what?" she exclaimed. Then she sat down with her son and talked about the evils of dishonesty.

"Now you must read every one of the books you were given credit for," she said.

"But, Mom," Jim replied, "those books are terrible. I'm not even interested in them."

No matter. Jim sat in his room for weeks, plugging away at *The Merchant of Venice* and *Romeo and Juliet,* while his friends played football outside his window. Finally, he came to the last book, a twelve-hundred-page rendition of *Ben Hur.* There he bogged down. He just couldn't finish that massive volume.

"Well then," said his mother, "you'll just have to go to your teacher and tell her what you've done."

Jim asked to see Mrs. Harris on the last day of school, and he confessed the whole miserable story to her. "But I just can't finish reading *Ben Hur*," he blurted out tearfully. Mrs. Harris forgave Jim, and the A+ was never removed from his record. In a sense, it was an unearned grade. In another, it was paid for in blood.

Reflecting on this episode today, Jim says with tongue in cheek, "I learned a lot from that experience. I learned not to tell my mother when I had done something wrong."

A year later, Jim was in the full bloom of adolescent giddiness. He was giving his teachers a hard time and earning academic marks barely above a C average. He got his one and only D—in high school or college—in shop class. On more than one occasion, he was sent to the principal's office where he received some stern lectures and a few "swats" with a notorious rubber hose. But these pressures were having no positive effect on his attitude or performance.

After watching her son's irresponsibility for a while, Myrtle went into action. One day after school she sat him down and said firmly, "I know that you have been fooling around in school and ignoring your assignments. I've thought it over, and I've decided that I'm not going to do anything about it. I'm not going to punish you. I'm not going to take away privileges. I'm not even going to talk about it anymore.

"I do want you to understand one thing, however," she continued. "If the principal ever calls *me* about your behavior, I promise you that the next day I'm going to school with you. I'm going to walk two feet behind you all day. I will hold your hand in front of all your friends in the hall and at lunch. I will sit as close to you as I can get during lunch, and I'm going to enter into all your conversations throughout the whole day. When you sit in your seat, I'm going to pull my chair up alongside you, or I'll climb into the seat with you. For one full day, I will not be away from your side."

Today Jim says of her threat, "I'm sure my teachers wondered why there was such a remarkable and sudden improvement in my behavior toward the end of my fifteenth year. It would have been social suicide for my mother to come to school! I couldn't run the risk of her fulfilling that awful promise."

By the time he was a senior in high school, Jim was an A student and on his way to a long academic career.

While Myrtle was a disciplinarian, she was also capable of extreme sensitivity to the needs of her son. They had just moved to San Benito, Texas, and she could see that Jim was feeling lonely and lost in this new setting. He had left his many friends behind in Bethany, Oklahoma.

Sensing her son's discomfort, Myrtle drew alongside him and pressed a twenty-dollar bill in his hand—an extremely generous gift at that time, and one which the Dobsons could not really afford.

"Spend it on anything you want," she told him. Although the money did not remove the longing for his old friends, it spoke volumes about his mother's concern for him. He never forgot it.

Many years later, he would reciprocate that tangible love by caring for her after the death of James, Sr. In fact, that provision was a fulfilled prophecy of sorts. One night in 1977, James, Sr. and Myrtle were going out for the evening. He was already dressed and was lying on the bed while she was getting ready. When she turned to look at him, she noticed his eyes were filled with tears.

"Why are you crying?" she asked.

"The Lord just spoke to me," he responded. "It's the strangest thing. I was just lying here watching you. I wasn't praying or even contemplating any serious thoughts. Then the Lord told me that He's going to take care of you." Neither of them understood the meaning of the revelation.

Three days later, James, Sr. had his first heart attack. Seventy-one days later he died. Myrtle was a widow at the age of sixty-eight and experienced such profound grief that it eventually took her life as well. But God kept the promise He had made that night to her beloved husband.

Jim had worried about his parents' financial situation. His father was a soft touch for anyone in need. Throughout his life he continued to give generously to the church. He seemed unaware that retirement years were coming when he would no longer be able to work. What would they live on? How would they survive?

Myrtle's financial needs were to be even greater than most pensioners. Her monthly allowance from her husband's pension fund was only $58 in 1977 and $84 by the time of her death in 1988. She required twenty-four-hour nursing care for the final five years of her life, at a cost of $50,000 annually. How would this obligation be met? The Lord had solved that problem back in 1977. Some stock in the Coca-Cola bottling company that Jim, Sr. had inherited from his father began to escalate in value. Through its dividends and later its sale, every bill was paid with money left over at the time of Myrtle's death. Truly, the fishes and the loaves had been broken and multiplied once more.

In 1980 Myrtle moved to Southern California where she could be close to her son and his family. Every Friday almost without fail, Jim took her to lunch. He listened carefully as she expressed her feelings and desires. He brought a pen and pad to these weekly sessions and made "To Do" lists based on her concerns. Then, in spite of his hectic schedule, he would pursue every assignment on that list until his mother's needs were met.

Although she enjoyed many happy moments with her grandchildren during the ensuing years, the loss of her beloved husband cast a pall over her that never lifted. Eventually, her deep grief had a debilitating effect on her physical health as well. Her condition was diagnosed as Parkinson's disease, and a search began for a special facility where she could receive around-the-clock nursing care.

After trying several convalescent homes that were inadequate to provide the medical treatment Myrtle required, the Dobsons finally found The House of Naomi in Pasadena, California. This home was a gift from God because it was run by a family of Christian women who lovingly took care of their patients. By this time, Myrtle could neither talk nor move. She was fed intravenously. Yet, every time the Dobsons visited the home, her hair was washed, her fingernails were manicured, and someone was hovering nearby to attend to her needs.

This loving care helped to ease the Dobsons' suffering as they helplessly watched Myrtle deteriorate. Those of us who worked closely with Dr. Dobson during this time observed his private suffering, but there was nothing we could do but pray. He often returned from his frequent visits feeling deeply discouraged.

Sometimes his phone would ring in the middle of a conversation, and he would pick it up to learn that his mother's condition had worsened or that the state medical bureaucracy was trying to force Myrtle out of The House of Naomi.

One Sunday afternoon a brief breakthrough came in Myrtle's situation, and Dr. Dobson recorded his thoughts on the pocket tape recorder he invariably carries.

Shirley and I just visited my mother in the nursing home where she resides. She has been rather deeply into senility in recent weeks and has been unable to either understand what we say or communicate with us. Yet today, the Lord granted us a brief reprieve. She was asleep when we arrived, and we gently sat on her bedside and awakened her.

She instantly recognized us, and for the first time in weeks, she was able to express her thoughts and understand the love that we gave to her. I took that opportunity, not knowing if it would return, to stroke her forehead and pat her hand and thank her for being a good mother. I thanked her for being a good wife to my father—a good pastor's wife, even though it was he who was called to the ministry.

I thanked her for living according to the principles of Christianity and staying true to the Christ whom she accepted when she was twenty-three years old. I stroked her face and thanked her for sacrificing to help me through college, doing without things that she needed. I thanked her for coming to our house when we were on our honeymoon and putting twenty dollars worth of groceries and staples in our cupboard when I knew she didn't have those same items in hers.

I told her how she was loved, not only by us, but by the Lord Himself. She smiled—she understood. She took my hand and said, "You know I've been thinking that it's almost over. I've almost made it. It's almost done."

I said, "Mom, when you make that crossing, you know my dad is going to be waiting for you on the other side." She smiled and understood.

Then I said, "Jesus is waiting for you, too. And He's going to say, 'Well done, thou good and faithful servant!'"

Then I prayed for her and thanked the Lord for the influence of a good woman and for her love in my life. She returned our love, and we said good-bye. At this stage of life, we never know when the last opportunity to communicate soul to soul has occurred. If this proves to be that final window of opportunity, I am grateful for the Lord's presence in that room today.

In fact, it was her final moment of lucid conversation with her son. She struggled on in a semi-comatose condition for nearly two more years. Then Myrtle went home to be with her Lord. During her waning hours on earth, Dr. Dobson recorded his thoughts about the life she lived and the heritage she had imparted to him. He shared those sentiments in a letter written the evening after he had been to her empty condominium.

As I sit down to write this letter tonight, I wonder if I have the right to put my thoughts into words. What I want to say is almost too intimate—too personal—to share even with my friends. And yet, I know that many of you feel very close to Shirley and me and the ministry of Focus on the Family. Some of you have told us that you include us in your prayers every day and almost think of us as members of your family. With that encouragement, then, I will risk making myself vulnerable by opening a window to my soul.

Perhaps you are aware that my mother is suffering from end-stage Parkinson's disease and will soon pass from this world to the next. She is totally paralyzed, is fed through a tube and lies in a fetal position within a darkened room. She no longer even recognizes the beloved members of her family. In her last coherent words spoken to me nearly two years ago, she expressed her desire to finish the course and meet her Savior and then her husband on the other side. We are praying that the final hour will come soon.

Knowing that my mother will never return to her little condominium near our home, Shirley and I set about sorting out and distributing her belongings a few days ago. We had dreaded this responsibility for many months. It is not easy to draw the curtain on a lifetime, but the task had to be done. There in pretty boxes and drawers and cabinets were the carefully organized remnants of more than seven decades of living. Faded photographs, cherished Christmas and birthday cards, meaningful letters and diaries told an incredible story of love and anguish for the man she married and then lost—my good father.

It is clear from the record that Myrtle Dillingham did not quickly fall in love with the lanky artist who pursued her in the spring of 1933. He, on the other hand, was captivated by this pretty brunette from the moment he first saw her. She toyed with him throughout their courtship, never sure whether she cared for him or not. Then one fateful evening, she pressed him too far. My father, being a proud man, walked out of her parents' home where she lived, never intending to return. He was a block away when he heard the sound of bare feet running toward him from behind. It was my mother who had suddenly had a change of heart. She loved him intensely from that night to the end of their lives together, some forty-three years later. My goodness, how she loved him!

What a godly man my father was. One of his dear friends, Rev. Noble Hathaway, came to visit Shirley and me this past spring. He told us many stories about my parents during the time of their first pastorate. He indicated that Dad was known in the little town of Sulphur Springs, Texas, as "the man with no leather on the toes of his shoes." It was true. He wore out the toes before the sole because he spent so much time on his knees in prayer. At twenty-four years of age, he felt totally inadequate to lead his flock unless he spent many hours every day in communion with God. The Lord must have been listening, because He blessed my father's ministry abundantly throughout the next forty-two years.

While sorting through the personal memorabilia in Mom's condo, we found a detailed account of their early years in that small Texas pastorate. My father received 55¢ after preaching his first sermon and averaged $8.00 per Sunday for the next fifty-two weeks. He led eighteen people into a personal relationship with Jesus Christ during those twelve months. (I wonder where those believers are today.) He was paid $1.00 for presiding over his first funeral. He earned a total of $429.82 during that initial year in the ministry and, remarkably, gave $352.00 back to the church. He and my mother lived on a small inheritance that came to them after my grandfather died in 1935. Throughout their lives together, they would give more than they could afford to the cause of Christ or to anyone who appeared to be more needy than they.

Speaking of finances, I was surprised to learn from my parents' tax records that they earned $60.00 per week in 1949 when my father was teaching college, and paid only $2.70 of that amount in federal income tax. That's right! The IRS extracted only 4.5 percent from the salary of a middle-class wage earner, which meant my mother never had to work outside the home.

Time and space do not permit me to tell the entire story of the intervening years, except to say that the love affair between these two devoted people continued uninterrupted for more than four decades. But all too quickly it was over. There within my mother's diary we found her account of my father's last full day on earth. He had suffered a massive heart attack some seventy days before but seemed to be recovering. He had recently been released from the hospital and was enjoying life to the fullest. Nevertheless, Mom lived in terror that her husband would suddenly be taken from her. She would not let him out of her sight for fear he would be stricken again. He chafed a bit under this scrutiny but usually yielded to his wife's anxieties. This is what she wrote to the memory of her husband exactly twelve months after his death.

My precious darling. One year ago today you spent your last day on this earth. One year ago we spent our last night together. I have recalled our concluding activities throughout this day. You wanted to go to the shopping center to take your daily walk, although I thought you really wanted to look at the fishing rods. We window-shopped for a while and then you said, "Myrtle, you *have* to let go of me. Let me be free to go in and out of the stores by myself . . . just to wander about free and alone." I took your arm and said, "Go where you want but let me go with you. Just let me walk beside you." For nearly three months I had been with you constantly. I seemed to know that you were to be taken from me suddenly, and I wanted to be there—perchance I could do something to keep you alive. But a few minutes later you said, "Look down this long mall. You can see to its end. I want to walk down there and back again." With that, I relented. But wouldn't you know, you took an escalator to one of the upper floors of the mall, removing you from my line of sight. Frantically, I finally found you coming toward me with a grin on your face. You took me to a furniture store on the third floor and showed me a new chair which you had selected for my Christmas gift. It was your last day. Your last big fling.

The following afternoon my father suddenly crossed the chilly waters of death. This is how Mother described his passing:

On Sunday, December 4, you dressed early and then went downstairs to sit in your chair. I spent the morning upstairs. I wonder what you did those two hours? I know you read the Bible . . . what else? If I'd come down, you would have talked to me about it. Later we went to Bud's house [their nephew] in Kansas City. You looked so handsome in your sportscoat and beige slacks. I sat saying nothing, just watching you manipulate your long arms, legs and body. You held the baby . . . not too gracefully . . . since it was never easy for you to hold an infant. At the table, you sat by me and told a funny story about us. Then your head and arm touched the table. They laid you on the floor. Bud breathed for you. He said you smiled once . . . your only sign of life. What did you see? Where did you go? My only comfort is that your last act on this earth was to lean toward me.

You had said in the past, "When I'm sick, I know you'll do everything possible to make me well. You'll know what to do . . .
who to call." I know I kept you alive again and again. But, my
darling, I couldn't save you this time. You went so quickly. I
wanted to be near you, but they wouldn't let me. Others were
trying to save you . . . but you slipped away.

The years that followed were marked by indescribable grief and
loneliness for my dear mother. She simply could not cope with his
passing. Her writings during those painful years are devastating to
read today. I sat on the living room floor in her condo and wept as I
comprehended, perhaps for the first time, the depths of her love and
her loss. These are her words:

> One day I realized that he did not exist anymore. His name
> was removed from the church register. The bank took his name
> off our checks. Our home address was rewritten to include only
> my name. His driver's license was invalidated. He was no more.
> Then I recognized that my name had changed, too. I had been
> proud to be Mrs. James C. Dobson, Sr. Now I was simply Myrtle
> Dobson. I was not *we* any longer. I became me or I. And I am
> alone. He was my high priest. Inside I'm broken, sad, stunned,
> alone. My house has lost its soul. He is not here!

Shortly thereafter, the appearance of physical symptoms resulted in a five-day stint for her in the hospital as a medical team
searched for a diagnosis. Two physicians then visited her bedside
to say, "It's not your physical ailments that are destroying you. It's
your grief and sorrow. And it will kill you if you cannot release
it." She couldn't. She never did. She loved too deeply, and her life
was too entwined with her man to ever extricate herself from his
memory. Some would see a contradiction in this inability to harmonize her dependence on God with her emotional and romantic
needs. I do not. God was the author of my mother's love for my
father, and He melted the two of them into "one flesh." I do not
believe He blamed her for those deep longings for my dad and
the life they had shared together. Remember that Adam enjoyed
the company of the Creator in the cool of the day, yet God pro-
nounced his situation "not good" and crafted a human companion
to meet his needs. In Mom's case, her specially designed companion was named James C. Dobson, Sr.

My mother's writings continued throughout the long months, including this note I found on simple yellow pad:

People have told me that the first year was the hardest. It's been one year and three days since you died, and tonight I am *frantic* with longing for you. Oh dear God! It's more than I can bear. The sobs make my heart skip beats. I cannot see the paper. My head throbs. The house is lonely and still. Visions of you have been as real as if you were here and had not left me. Today I thanked God for letting an angel watch over me. But how desperately I missed you!

It is very cold outside. Last night, a sleet storm covered the earth with ice and then froze into a solid crust. The streets are slippery and dangerous. I hate it. It makes me feel blue, frightened, and alone. I dread the winter to follow. It will last for three more months.

I moved into the smaller bedroom today. I wish you were here to share that room with me. There are precious memories there. When I was ill four years ago, you prayed for me in that bedroom during the midnight hours. You lay on the floor, agonizing in prayer for me. We both knew the Spirit was praying through you. Later, the Lord led us to a doctor who helped me find my way back to health. Oh how I loved you. I love your memory today.

She continued:

Benji [my father's little terrier] misses you too. He sits on the bed with ears pointed upward. His eyes are fixed on the stairs. Sometimes he growls. Sometimes he barks loudly. Sometimes he walks to the head of the stairs and stands motionless, as if he expects someone. He is puzzled by your absence.

In 1980, Mother moved to Pasadena, California, to be near Shirley, the kids, and me. She found solace in the Bible in those years and seemed to struggle to her feet, momentarily. For example, she wrote in her diary on December 10, 1980, that the Lord had given her some Scripture in the middle of the night. One of the verses she loved was as follows:

I tell you the truth, you will weep and mourn while the world rejoices. You will grieve, but your grief will turn to joy. A woman giving birth to a child has pain because her time has come; but when her baby is born she forgets the anguish because of her joy that a child is born into the world. So with you: Now is your time of grief, but I will see you again and you will rejoice, and no one will take away your joy (John 16:20–22 NIV).

44

My mother obviously held tightly to these promises of God throughout her final years of struggle, especially those relating to eternal life. They are precious to me, too. Because of the anticipation of life beyond the grave, Myrtle Dobson's story will not end in tragedy. It will conclude with a shout of victory! That wretched bed that has held her captive will no longer be able to possess her. The tubes and bandages and medications will fall aside, and she will be swept into the loving arms of the Savior whom she has served so faithfully since she was a girl. You can be sure my father will be there on that day, too. He will embrace her in one of the great reunions of all time. And they will be forever with the Lord.

[Two days later]

What joy I have to share with you, my friends. The thoughts expressed above were written in the middle of the night on June 26, 1988. I began rereading my mother's diaries and writing down my observations at 11:00 P.M., and finally put down my pen at 4:00 A.M. It seemed that the presence of the Lord hovered near me as I wrote into the early hours of the morning. I had intended to say so much more but was eventually overtaken by sleep. I wanted to share some ideas and understandings that occurred to me while I was considering my mother's writings . . . reflecting on the brevity of life, the folly of materialism, and the all-consuming importance of serving the Lord with all our hearts, minds, and strength. I wanted to urge my readers to love their families while they can—guarding against petty disagreements and irritations that might stand in the way. There is so much on my heart, but those perspectives will have to wait.

I stumbled into bed in the early morning light and arose three hours later to attend Sunday services at our local church. That afternoon (yesterday) our daughter came by for a brief visit and read the letter I had written earlier that morning. Danae was deeply moved by what she learned about her grandmother, and we stood misty-eyed and talked about the love we shared for the woman we called "Myrna." As God is my witness, the phone rang at that precise moment. It was a nurse at the convalescent home where my mother was a patient. She told us that Mom had died at 4:45 P.M. that afternoon. She had taken one last breath, then quietly slipped into eternity.

Myrtle Georgia Dillingham Dobson is now safely in the arms of Jesus, where she will experience no more suffering, no more tears, no more disease, no more pain, no more loneliness, no more grief, no more separation, and no more death. Praise the Lord! Her spirit is free, never again to be shackled in the sinful world. The joy and grandeur that she is experiencing today cannot be expressed in human terms. Do I, you ask, *really* believe in this "hope of glory" beyond the grave for those who have been covered by the blood of the Lamb? You bet I do—with every fiber of my being! I have banked everything of value to me on the certainty of that promise. Isaiah laid it out for us in unmistakable terms: "Yet we have this assurance: Those who belong to God shall live again. Their bodies shall rise again! Those who dwell in the dust shall awake and sing for joy! For God's light of life will fall like dew upon them!" (Isa. 26:19 TLB). What a magnificent promise at a time of separation and loss like we face today!

Good-bye, Mom. What a great wife and mother you were. We will miss you terribly. I draw comfort today from the fact that you and I have closed out our time on earth with no regrets and no bad memories to be suppressed. There were no bitter words, no wounded pride, nothing for which to apologize or seek forgiveness. Nothing has transpired between us but unmitigated love. How sweet is your passing from this life to the next. Give my dad a hug for me, won't you? Tell him I'm trying to carry on the work he left behind. And yes, tell him to look for our little family on that great resurrection morning. We *will* be there. I promise you that! We *will* be there!

4

Four Men Who Shaped His Life

While James Dobson's parents instilled in him a sense of moral character and a heart for God, four men he met in college were particularly significant forces in shaping his professional life. Their influence helped Jim integrate his Christian principles with his education and ultimately directed him into his career.

Upon graduation from high school in San Benito, Texas, in 1954, he headed west to Southern California. He enrolled in Pasadena College, a Christian liberal arts school, which has since been relocated to San Diego and renamed Point Loma University.

It was at this age that his father had struggled so desperately with the call to preach. But Jim heard no inner voice. Despite the family tradition (he was preceded on his mother's side by three generations of preachers), he felt no pressure from either his parents or his Lord to pursue a career in the ministry.

During his freshman year in college, he studied under two of the four mentors who would so dramatically affect his future. The first was Dr. Eddie Harwood, a professor of English who taught creative writing for the more talented students. Jim had not intended to take the notoriously tough class, but he was assigned to it because he had scored high marks on an entrance exam. When he learned of Dr. Harwood's reputation as a tough disciplinarian, Jim approached him and asked for a transfer. "I don't think I am capable of doing the work in your class," he told Dr. Harwood. What he really meant was that he didn't *want* to work that hard.

The professor had heard every excuse through the years, and he wasn't going to buy this one. "I will not approve your transfer," he told the freshman. "You'll see that you *will* be able to do the work, and I will want you in my class."

Indeed, the freshman composition course turned out to be the most profitable academic experience of Jim's undergraduate training. It is true that he worked much harder than he had intended, and there were times when he thought he would not survive. Dr. Harwood was as tough as nails and twice as sharp.

"I can't teach you how to write," he told the class. "But I can sure teach you how *not* to write. You try it, and I'll tell you what you've done wrong."

The professor gave the students assignments designed to draw out corny colloquialisms and syrupy sentimentality. He then massacred their compositions, spreading red ink everywhere, and topping them off prominently with D's and F's. It was a grueling experience, but slowly the principles of sentence structure and good writing began to come alive. The students were learning how to write, but more importantly, they were learning how to *think*.

Not only did Jim survive that experience, but he thrived on it. He earned an A that semester and proceeded to take three more classes from Dr. Harwood. The last one was entitled "Advanced Exposition" and was designed specifically for Dobson and three other talented students. Today, he credits Dr. Harwood not only with teaching him how to use the English language, but with transforming him from a high school pupil into a college student in that one freshman class. Harwood went on to become a vice-president of one of the University of California schools, and he has stayed in touch with his former student.

Dr. Harwood might appreciate knowing that his legacy is alive and well today at Focus on the Family. It is common for those who work with Dr. Dobson to receive his editorial comments written—Harwood style—all over their drafts of articles, memos, and correspondence. He often points out weak transitions or tangential thoughts with his editor's pen. Sometimes he finds it easier simply to fix the problem himself rather than to explain it. In those instances, his staff is accustomed to having their papers returned with entirely new paragraphs written in the margins. If Dobson deems a project to be unsalvageable, he typically labels it across the top with the kiss of death: "sophomoric writing."

The structured approach to writing that he learned from Dr. Harwood also manifests itself in a curious method that Dobson uses to this day. Because all of his writing must flow in a direct line from point A to point B, he writes with a pencil on yellow legal pads and then tapes the sheets together to form a continuous scroll. If a particular illustration seems out of place, he simply snips the section out and tapes it in somewhere else.

I remember one morning in 1987 when he returned to town after a long writing trip. He came to my office and asked me to hold one end of the scroll he had written. He then began backing down the hallway, unrolling the manuscript to *Love for a Lifetime* as he walked. It must have stretched fifty feet!

His publishers have tried to convince him that using a word processor would be more efficient. But Dobson likes the thoughts to flow directly from his mind to the paper, with no keyboard or electronic screen to interfere with the creative process.

The writing skills Dobson learned in his college composition classes had application to his other academic courses as well. They were particularly helpful in his psychology classes, where he encountered another intellectual "giant," Dr. Paul Culbertson, who became his major professor and mentor for years to come. Dr. Culbertson recalls a seventy-page report Dobson wrote comparing various theories of neuroses. "When I read that paper," he said, "I knew this young man had a future in psychology."

During his first year in college, Dobson was relatively certain he wanted to be a psychologist. Culbertson's teaching had opened his mind to the fascinating studies of human behavior. By his third year in college, he was on a track headed toward a Ph.D. and a career in the field of mental health. From that moment on, he never wavered from his course. Like his father,

Jim was something of a guided missile. Once he knew his target, he was totally committed to the pursuit of it.

His plans at this point in life also called for getting married, having children, and buying a home. But then he had an encounter with a third influential educator whose advice helped him to zero in on the goal he had established for himself. His aunt Lela London had heard a Christian psychologist named Clyde Narramore speak one day, and he offered to spend an afternoon with any promising student who wanted to enter the field of mental health.

"We need Christians in this work," he said, "and I'll help those who are interested." Dr. Narramore was a pioneer in Christian psychology. Prior to his time, behavioral studies had been widely regarded by evangelicals as a field for practicing atheists. From his aunt, Jim learned of the open invitation and decided to take advantage of it.

"I called Dr. Narramore a few days later, and he graciously agreed to see me," Dobson recalls. "This busy man gave me two hours of his time in the living room of his home. Thirty years later I still remember his words. Among other things, he warned me not to get married too quickly if I wanted to earn a Ph.D. and become a practicing psychologist.

"He said, 'A baby will come along before you know it, and you will find yourself under financial pressure. That will make you want to quit. You'll sit up nights caring for a sick child and then spend maybe $300 in routine medical bills. Your wife will be frustrated, and you will be tempted to abandon your dreams. Don't put yourself in that straitjacket.'"

As a result of this counsel, Dobson postponed marriage until he was twenty-four years old, and he and Shirley waited years beyond that to have their first child. While it is typical today for couples to start families at a later stage in life, in the 1960s it was highly unusual. This late start explains why Dobson was, in his words, "the oldest living father of a teenager."

Jim's decision to follow Dr. Narramore's advice caused some external stress. All the Dobsons' friends, it seemed, were having children and getting on with the business of raising families. It didn't help matters when some of these well-meaning peers began to apply a little pressure to Jim and Shirley. One night when

51

the Dobsons were entertaining friends, the good-natured teasing went a little too far. They began to get insulting about the Dobsons' "barrenness."

That provoked an angry response from Jim who told the group he had reached his limit. He angrily struck back at everyone in the room, telling them if they wanted his friendship they had better back off. Shirley later recalled that his retort was like a bomb dropped in the middle of the party. "Our guests scattered to every room of the house just to get out of his line of fire."

That was fine with Jim. He and Shirley knew what they were doing, and he didn't intend to let his friends deter them.

It was that singleness of purpose that made such an impression on Dr. Narramore. One day in 1988 he visited Focus on the Family to see his protégé, and he told me, "I can vividly recall the day that Jim came to see me. He made such an impression on me that I can even remember what he was wearing that day! He was different from many other students seeking my career counsel because he was so sincere. I knew he'd go far."

Earlier in his college career, Jim had intended to pursue his graduate studies at the University of Texas. This was a natural choice since he had grown up in that state and it would bring him closer to his parents and family.

But one afternoon he had a conversation with Dr. Ken Hopkins, the fourth mentor who left his mark on Jim Dobson. Dr. Hopkins had graduated from Pasadena College three years earlier and had just earned his Ph.D. from the University of Southern California. Jim had called him about a research project, and near the end of their conversation, Hopkins asked Jim about his plans for graduate studies.

"Why don't you consider USC?" Hopkins asked. "Come on down here and let me show you around."

Jim accepted his offer and eventually decided to enroll at the university, which was located near downtown Los Angeles. The decision was life changing because a move to Texas would have taken him away from Shirley at a crucial time in their relationship.

On the night of enrollment at USC, Jim wasn't so sure he had made the right decision. He was more than a little apprehensive about being on the huge campus. He felt lost among the twenty thousand students registering for classes, and he wondered if his faith would be respected in that university. Suddenly a familiar face appeared. In that mass of humanity, Dr. Hopkins found him and put his arm around his shoulder. He invited Jim up to his office and told him he believed in him and then offered to serve as his major professor.

"He was like an angel that the Lord put in my path at a precise moment," Dr. Dobson recalls. "He understood and shared my faith, and he guided me through the next five years. He was my advisor on research. He told me which classes to take and which to avoid. I will always be grateful to God for placing Dr. Ken Hopkins there at such an important time in my life."

With this guidance, Jim was able to graduate with precisely the number of units needed for his degree. On April 3, 1967, he received a Ph.D. in Child Development and a minor in Research Design. In five years of graduate study, he had earned straight A's, with the exception of three B's, giving him a graduate GPA of 3.91. The guided missile had found its target.

Many years have passed since those early days of training and career development, but Dobson has not forgotten the roles those four men played in shaping him. Their influence was incalculable; without it, he would be a much different person today.

Reflecting today on Dobson's relationships with these four compassionate professionals, one theme emerges—the value of older, more established men and women who are willing to give their time and energy to impressionable members of the younger generation. Dr. Narramore devoted only two short hours to a promising student one afternoon, and yet that investment reverberates down to this day. Focusing our energies on a leader of tomorrow might be the most important thing we'll do in a lifetime. Drs. Eddie Harwood, Paul Culbertson, Clyde Narramore, and Ken Hopkins are to be commended. They were there when it counted.

5

Romance, Thy Name Is Shirley Deere

When Jim was a twenty-one-year-old senior at Pasadena College, he began dating a twenty-year-old sophomore named Shirley Deere. She had been attracted to the tall (6'2"), blue-eyed Texan who was captain of the tennis team, but they had never met. Then one day, he had just finished a tennis match and was walking across campus in his tennis shorts. Shirley saw that their paths were going to cross, so she decided to introduce herself to him. But at the moment of truth, her heart started racing, and she became flustered. In a panic she suddenly blurted, "Hi, legs!"—painfully revealing her secret admiration for his lanky physique.

Their next encounter wasn't until the following summer. They both remained at school while most of their classmates headed home for the vacation break. From time to time they bumped into each other in the library, the cafeteria, and other spots around campus, but they rarely exchanged anything more than a brief greeting.

One night after the dinner meal on campus, Jim and Shirley found themselves standing near one another in a circle of friends. Capturing the moment, Jim sidled up to Shirley and said, "See this nickel? I'm gonna flip it in the air. If you can call heads or tails correctly, I'll buy you a hamburger. But if you lose, you'll owe me one."

How's that for a new approach? Jim would be a winner either way because he got a date out of the arrangement. Shirley liked the idea and said, "It's a deal." She called "heads" as the nickel went into the air, but it landed tails.

"Good," said Jim. "When do you want to pay off?"

"Hey, wait a minute!" Shirley protested. "Give me a fighting chance. Let's go double or nothing."

Jim flipped the coin and Shirley lost again.

"Great," said Jim. "I like hamburgers. Now I get two of them."

"Let's go one more time," she demanded.

Jim checked the nickel. "You now owe me four hamburgers," he said.

Before they had completed the game, Shirley owed him one hundred twenty-eight hamburgers, and she's been frying them ever since.

Shortly thereafter, Jim and Shirley had their first date. She was something of a socialite and had dated many young men, but she immediately observed that Jim was different from the others. He invited her to accompany him to a Sunday evening church service and dinner afterward. When he arrived at her dorm, he was dressed in a smart sport coat and matching slacks. That night, he treated her like a lady by opening doors for her, helping her with her coat, and introducing her to others. Following the service, he took her to a beautiful Italian restaurant in Hollywood. She noted how well he carried himself and how sophisticated he was. He spoke politely to the waiters and others who served them. His conversation was filled with humor and stories told in vivid detail.

She later discovered that he had learned these social skills from his parents, whose travels had placed him in many situations where proper etiquette was required. His parents had also taught him to respect women and to maintain high moral standards in his relationships with them. It did not escape Shirley's attention that he didn't even try to maneuver her toward a payoff kiss on their first date. In fact, he waited until the third date before he held her hand. And although he was something of a ladies' man, he had never told any girl that he loved her. He felt this was not a term to be thrown around casually, and he waited more than a year before confessing it to Shirley.

What was Jim Dobson like in college? Shirley will tell you that he was a very good tennis player. He won the school tournament his last two years and played the number one position on the team during his senior year. He was tall, athletic, known for his wit—and his temper. He was a good student his last two years and was an outstanding writer even then. He hung out with an "in-crowd" that was never quite happy with the way things were being run. Some people even considered him a rebel because he was mischievous and occasionally violated minor rules and regulations of the college. But his faith never wavered. He knew precisely who he was and where he was going.

Jim and Shirley had a wonderful college courtship throughout his senior and her sophomore year. It was almost like a storybook love affair, and Jim proved to be quite romantic and creative. One night after a date, he escorted Shirley to her dorm just before curfew. Shirley was still thirsty for a soft drink and, knowing she couldn't leave the dorm, she asked Jim if he could send a Coke to her room later on. Within a few minutes, her dorm mate (who had permission to be out late) delivered the bottle to Shirley. When she pried off the cap, she discovered a small piece of paper rolled up and inserted in the neck of the bottle. It was a love note he had written and placed there for her refreshment!

As the relationship grew, Shirley began to feel a need to tell him about her past. It is never easy for the children of alcoholic parents to reveal this embarrassing and hidden part of their lives. Shirley was no exception. She had buried the pain of her childhood beneath a pleasant exterior and revealed it to no one. Now, however, she began to be uncomfortable with her secret. She thought she was falling in love with Jim. Didn't he have a right to know who she really was? But how would he react to the news of her troubled roots? Could he be trusted? Would the truth destroy their relationship?

One evening as they sat talking together on campus, she gingerly broached the subject. "There is something I need to tell you," she began. "My childhood was not what you think it was. My father was an abusive alcoholic who made life miserable for my mother, my brother, and me. He drank up his paycheck every week, and we lived in poverty throughout my elementary school years. I've gone through so much pain . . ."

Shirley was crying by the time she told the entire story to her friend. Instead of reacting with shock, Jim put his arms around her and held her close. Realizing her vulnerability, he talked quietly with her for more than an hour. He assured her that rather than being repelled by the truth, it gave him an appreciation for who she was and the strength she had shown in overcoming her hardship. Shirley's revelation had actually drawn them closer to one another.

They dated steadily throughout Jim's senior year and up to the time of his graduation in May 1958. Then, Uncle Sam decided he wanted two years of Jim's life. The draft board called Jim for a physical examination, after which a tough-talking sergeant addressed those who had been selected. "Welcome to the army, men. You're the guys we want!"

Dobson reacted immediately. He had already planned to go to graduate school, and he had no desire to spend the next two years in military service. Thus, he rushed down and joined the National Guard, which required six months' active duty and five-and-one-half years of reserve training. That permitted him to continue his education with a delay of only six months.

Before he left for active duty, Jim and Shirley pledged themselves to be true to one another. He was assigned to basic training in Fort Ord, which was several hundred miles north of Pasadena. Jim would hitch a ride with his army buddies every time he could get a leave, and he and Shirley carried on a long-distance romance until the last day of that year. Then the long period of separation took its toll.

When Jim came home for Christmas vacation, they had a wonderful few days together. It was just like old times. Nevertheless, something was secretly bothering him, but he waited until the final hour of his leave before coming out with it. They had spent the entire day together on New Year's Eve and were sitting in Jim's car before saying good-night. Then he gave Shirley the shock of her life.

He said, "I've been doing a lot of thinking about our relationship, Shirls, and I'm concerned about it. You know I care about you, but I just don't believe I'm going to marry you. When I get out of the army, I'm going to graduate school at the University of Texas, and that could be the end for you and me. What worries me is that you're going to wait for me through your senior year and miss your opportunity to have a good time and find someone else. That's why I think you should start dating other people, and I'll do the same."

Shirley was stunned. She had no idea Jim was about to end the relationship, but her pride kept her from showing her inner desperation.

"Yes," she said. "I've been thinking the same thing. There are some guys on campus I've been interested in, and I'd like to date them while I'm in school. Let's do as you say."

Jim walked her to the door of the dorm and asked if he could kiss her good-bye.

"No," she replied. "Let's just shake on it," and she put out her hand. With that, Shirley went in the dorm and cried all night.

The ease with which she had let him go deeply upset Jim. Suddenly he didn't want to leave. He felt that he had hurt the best friend he ever had, and his desire to reverse his course began to well up inside. The next day, Jim drove the three hundred miles back to Fort Ord, in deep thought every inch of the way. When evening fell, he went to the phone and called his former sweetheart.

"I've made a big mistake," he told her. "I don't know what came over me, but I want you to forget what I said. I don't want anybody but you."

By this time Shirley was wary. Again, her instincts told her not to jump too quickly. She waited two full weeks before writing Jim, while he stewed and wondered if she would ever love him again. That period of contemplation—that time of doubt—was just what he needed to fall head over heels in love. For the first time in his life, he knew Shirley was the one. In nearly three decades he has not wavered from that decision.

How interesting it is that Jim later wrote a book for those who are rejected in love (*Love Must Be Tough*), based on the principles evident in his experiences with Shirley. He tested his hypothesis in many subsequent counseling sessions, confirming that the

Jim and Myrtle Dobson with their baby boy.

Jimmy in his first "Ford."

Shirley in her eighth year.

Three-year-old Jimmy with his father.

Sixteen years later.

Myrtle in Hawaii, 1956.

Collegiate hi-jinks! Jim and his friends stage a mock ballet for a Men's Revue, 1955.

Jim with his college tennis team, 1957. He played the #2 position that year, but won the school tournament.

Homecoming Queen at Pasadena College, 1960.

Jim and his cousin, H.B. London, during their senior year in college.

Myrtle Dobson in Alaska, 1957.

Jim with his mother, 1958.

Jim and Shirley with their parents on the wedding night, August 27, 1960. (Shirley's mother and stepfather left, and Jim's parents, right.)

Jim and Shirley leave for their honeymoon, 1960. "They had only just begun."
Jim's father is visible on the right.

Shirley with their newly purchased and beloved 1957 Ford.
The entire front end had just been rebuilt!

The Dobson's first home, purchased in 1964 for $21,900. They saved for two years to come up with the 10 percent down payment.

A photo of Shirley taken at 3AM when delivery appeared to be imminent. It wasn't!

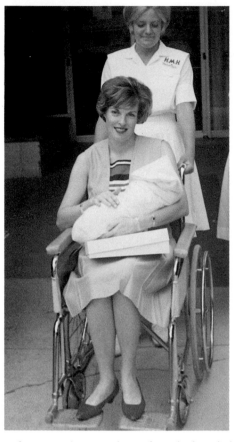

A new mother goes home from the hospital with her baby daughter, Danae Ann:

Graduation day at USC, June, 1967.

The proud new father with baby, Ryan, 1970.

Dr. Dobson receives an Honorary Doctorate of Laws degree from Pepperdine University, Malibu, California. Presenting the award are Dr. Michael Adams (left) and Dr. Howard White.

Dr. Dobson receives an Honorary Doctorate of Humanities from Franciscan University of Steubenville, Ohio. With him is university president Father Michael Scanlan.

Seattle Pacific University awards an Honorary Doctorate of Human Letters to Dr. Dobson. University President David LeShana (right) joins Dr. Dobson after the ceremony.

Photo by Eric Johnson

Jim and Shirley receive Honorary Doctorates from Asbury Theological Seminary in Wilmore, Kentucky, 1989.

Shirley contemplating 19,000 empty seats the afternoon before she and Jim were to speak in McNichols Arena, Denver.

Former Executive Vice President, David "Mac" McQuiston, prays for the Dobsons before they address the huge crowd in Denver.

An evening with Jim and Shirley Dobson in Phoenix, Arizona.

The Dobsons with Billy Graham during the Calgary, Alberta Crusade, 1983.

Shirley clowning for her photographer-husband in their back yard.

Rev. James Dobson a few months before his death in 1977.

Shirley on the USC campus in 1985.

A Christmas dinner being prepared by Shirley and her mother in Alma's kitchen.

Dr. Dobson interviews President Reagan in the Oval Office for an upcoming radio broadcast.

Dr. Dobson with President Reagan, Secretary of the Treasury, James Baker, and a team of citizens concerned about tax reform for families. This photograph was taken in the Cabinet Room of the White House, 1985.

best way to handle romantic rejection is to turn loose and pull backward as Shirley did. To hold on tightly in that moment of crisis is to risk killing the relationship. If Shirley had hung on Jim's neck that night and begged for his love, he might never have returned. Instinctively, from somewhere deep inside, she understood that concept and handled the challenge beautifully.

Jim was soon to be tested in a similar way. When he had fulfilled his military obligation, he enrolled at USC instead of going to Texas. He was now convinced that he wanted to marry Shirley, but suddenly she was unsure. Their roles had flip-flopped from his college days. Jim was no longer the big man on campus. He was a forgotten has-been, and Shirley was in her glory. She was elected homecoming queen and senior class president that spring and was later named to *Who's Who in American Colleges and Universities.* She was one of the most popular girls on campus and was pursued by many attractive men.

All this competition gave Jim an even greater desire to marry Shirley, and he found himself "chasing" her. The more he demanded her attention, the more distant she became. Her behavior was curious to him. For two years he had had this girl in the palm of his hand. Why, now, was she slipping away? True to his methodical nature, he sat down one day for more than two hours and thought about that riddle. Then it hit him! Of course! He was acting like a puppy dog waiting for Shirley to throw him a bone. No wonder she was treating him disrespectfully!

That day Jim mapped out a whole new plan for his approach to Shirley. He was going to project an image of security, strength, confidence, and independence. If she chose to walk away from him, he was prepared to let her go. Either way, he was through playing the role of a beggar.

The first night Jim put on the new persona, Shirley changed her attitude in a dramatic way. As they rode along in the car, she moved close and put her arms around him. "Would you pull over to the curb and stop the car?" she asked.

As Jim complied, she said, "I'm afraid I'm losing you and I don't know why." In the moonlight he saw tears in her eyes.

Jim gave Shirley a little speech that night, telling her he was going somewhere in life, and he hoped she would come along with him. But if she didn't want to join him, that was okay, too. He would just find someone else.

They were married a few months later.

In the days prior to the wedding, Jim again raised the issue of Shirley's difficult childhood. One evening, as they sat in his car laying plans for their lives, he shared something that had been on his mind.

"I want you to know that I am hereby pledging myself to your happiness as compensation for the years you lost at home," he said. "That will be one of my major objectives as your husband." And so it has been.

One thing was obvious as they approached married life. They needed a newer car. For years Jim had been driving a dilapidated heap he called "Ol' Red." This 1949 Mercury convertible was a disaster on wheels. The top wouldn't go up or down, the electric windows didn't work, the lights sometimes went out unexpectedly, and the engine dozed off every now and then. Jim never knew if he would get where he was going. A typical scene around town was Shirley steering the wreck while Jim pushed it. Once they got it started, people would drive alongside and point frantically at the wheels, which appeared to be falling off. It was a humiliating experience.

Furthermore (and most frustrating to Shirley), the front seat of the car was disintegrating. Springs stuck up at various angles, snagging her clothes and puncturing her backside. Shirley *hated* that car with a passion, but Jim didn't want to go into debt to buy a newer one. Tension was obviously brewing between Dobson and Deere over the pile of junk he used to transport her.

This conflict culminated one day as Jim came to the dorm to get Shirley. They had scheduled important job interviews that day, and she had spent two hours getting dressed. She was wearing her best outfit—a black suit she had just retrieved from the cleaners. So off they went. As they flew down the road at fifty miles per hour, the rotted old convertible top suddenly blew off. Bits of string and canvas beat them about the head and shoulders, and dust settled everywhere. The remnants of the top hooked onto the back of the car and flapped outward like Superman's cape.

Shirley had absolutely had enough. She screamed at Jim from

the floorboard, where she crouched to escape the flogging. Jim was angry, too, not just at his car but at Shirley. For Pete's sake! It wasn't *his* fault. So he just kept on driving, with the ribs of his convertible top glistening in the sun, the ragged canvas flapping out the back, and his fianceé yelling at him from under the dashboard. Passersby must surely have thought these folks were crazy.

Given this background, it was a minor triumph for Shirley to get Jim to agree to buy a newer car. They picked out a gleaming, white, 1957 Ford with white sidewall tires and a hard top. They drove Ol' Red up to the used car lot, where the engine sighed once and gave up the ghost. Somewhere in a salvage yard sits a lonely red Mercury with no top. On a spring protruding from the front seat are tiny woolen fibers ripped from a co-ed's skirt.

But that inconvenience was finally over for them. Jim and Shirley climbed into their shiny new (three-year-old) car and patted the dashboard. They could not have been more proud if they had just bought a new Rolls Royce. Down the road they drove in their chariot, feeling like a king and queen. They had gone only five blocks when Jim leaned over and kissed Shirley to celebrate the happy moment, but just as he did, the two cars in front of them made an unexpected stop in the middle of the block. Jim was on top of them by the time he looked up. He slammed on the brakes, but it was too late.

The events of the next few seconds have been preserved in their minds like an old videotape. "I can still hear my tires screeching and then the awful sounds of metal crunching against metal and breaking glass tinkling as it fell to the pavement," Jim recalls. "I can see the hood and fenders of my beautiful car rising in slow motion toward me. At the same time, Shirley and I are falling forward as our heads hit the sun visors."

It was actually a three-car collision since Jim knocked one car into the next in line. Fortunately, no one was hurt. The stunned couple got out of the car and surveyed the wreckage. They were sick over what they had done. Moreover, they were afraid someone might have seen the careless kiss that caused the accident. They weren't afraid to admit their fault in the matter; they just didn't want the whole world to know that an untimely kiss was really to blame.

While Jim was exchanging information with the two irritated drivers, Shirley overheard two little boys talking on the sidewalk.

"What happened?" one of the lads asked.

"Oh, that guy over there kissed the girl and hit two cars in front of him," the other responded matter-of-factly. Shirley held her breath!

Then the boys rode off on their bicycles, thereby concealing, until this moment, the embarrassing truth.

Although the damages were covered by Jim's insurance policy, he had to reckon with a $100 deductible—precisely the amount they were planning to spend for Shirley's wedding ring. On the wedding night she had to settle for a silver band, but Jim surprised her on their first anniversary with the ring she should have received twelve months earlier.

They were married on August 27, 1960, with James, Sr. officiating at the wedding. After a brief honeymoon, they returned to their small apartment and began their new life together. Those were wonderful days for the newlyweds, but they were not without some measure of hardship.

"Every bride dreams of the romantic marriage with picnics in the park, weekend dates, and bouquets of flowers," Shirley says. "We were deeply in love, but the first years of our marriage were not easy ones. When we returned from our honeymoon, we only had $100 in our bank account. We were expecting our first checks from our new jobs within five weeks, but until they arrived, we survived on pork and beans. That was the least expensive meal I knew of. I served up pork and beans with brown bread, pork and beans with hot dogs, and pork and beans with tortillas!"

They both began teaching in elementary school that year; Jim taught the sixth grade and Shirley taught the second. They worked late almost every night in their apartment, grading papers and making charts and bulletin boards. On more than one occasion, they fell asleep on the living room floor with their papers spread around them. There the exhausted couple would sit until the wee hours of the morning when one of them would awaken and they would drag themselves off to bed.

In addition to teaching, Jim was working hard to complete his master's degree. "On weekends," Shirley recalls, "Jim spent long hours studying. I was a good sport about it, but the sacrifices were not fun. All our friends were fixing up their homes, going out for dinner, and having children."

Jim must have sensed the strain this was putting on Shirley. One night, shortly after he had begun his doctoral program, he announced that he had reached an important decision. "I know these have been difficult days for you, Shirley," he said. "We've been pushing so hard to get my degree, but I believe it is beginning to interfere with our marriage. Nothing is worth that price. I've decided to take some time off so you and I can spend more time with each other."

The significance of that decision was not lost on Shirley. She knew that a postponement of his graduate degree represented a tremendous sacrifice for the career-minded student she had married.

"I will always love and respect Jim for making that choice," Shirley says now. "I will never forget it."

This seemed to validate an assessment made by Jim's aunt, Lela London, who had told Shirley during the engagement that she was making a wise decision to marry him. "The Dobson men make wonderful family men," she had confided to Shirley. "You won't regret marrying Jim."

Indeed, Shirley has never regretted that decision. While making it clear that Jim has his full share of flaws and shortcomings, she speaks warmly about the characteristics that drew her to him.

"First, he is one of the most generous men I've ever known," she says. "If you are really in need, you can have about anything he has—except his food when he's hungry. He has never permitted me to pick tasty bites off his plate, and of course, I love to do that. But he has always been willing to share his resources with those around him. I remember when we were first married, he looked ahead to a time when our parents would be getting older and perhaps financially dependent on us. He wanted to make sure we had a standing agreement about that situation, regardless of which set of folks were in need.

"He said to me, 'Let it be understood that we will do whatever is necessary to take care of them in that hour, whether they're on your side of the family or mine. We must always treat them with love and dignity. Someday we will lose them, and I want no regrets or guilt when that moment comes.'

"Jim has also been generous with the church. He is a strong believer in tithing and has never earned a dollar in his life that he did not share with God's work. Likewise, he has been a good steward of the family resources.

"I wasn't terribly materialistic when we married," Shirley continues, "but I didn't see a problem with credit buying. I probably would have made the same mistake many young couples make by going into debt to purchase appliances and furniture. But I accepted Jim's leadership in this area, and he believed in cash purchases."

As a result of her husband's careful budgeting, they never had to live under the black cloud of debt. Those of us who work closely with Dr. Dobson today can attest to this aspect of his philosophy. Focus on the Family has never missed a payroll, never deliberately paid an invoice late and has never gone heavily into debt—all as a result of its founder's conservative approach to money management.

Shirley was also impressed with Jim's deep commitment to their church. In retrospect, the fact that he took her to a Sunday evening service on their first date seems appropriate. "Jim almost never misses church if he is at home," she says. "Even when he returns from a long trip at one o'clock on a Sunday morning, he will usually get up and go to Sunday school. I know he has been dead on his feet from fatigue, but he has never wanted his children to see him staying at home on a Sunday morning or night."

Then Shirley adds, "Another thing that drew me to Jim was his wonderful sense of humor. Even on our first few dates back in 1957, he made me laugh more than any guy I had dated. I loved that about him. He had a very clever way of seeing the world around him, and his graphic descriptions were legendary at the college we attended. That is one reason Jim has been a good writer and speaker.

"We still love to laugh together twenty-nine years later. I think that has helped us to cope with the pressures we have experienced. We have so much fun together. Just last week we were flying home from a conference, and I had set a glass of tomato juice on the armrest between us. We both forgot it was there, and Jim knocked it off on my side. Within seconds, my skirt and sweater looked like they were soaked in blood.

"I guess it was my predicament that struck us funny—having to get off the plane looking like I'd been in a knife fight. Jim especially got a good chuckle out of it. But while he was laughing with his eyes shut, I poured the other half of the tomato juice in his lap. I know it was a crazy thing to do, but I did it on impulse. He was still chuckling when the cold juice soaked through to the skin. Then the shock hit him, and the two of us laughed until we had tears in our eyes. The flight attendant wondered how one glass of tomato juice could cover two people so completely.

"We walked off the plane looking like we'd attacked each other with chain saws. We don't do wild things like that every day, but we do find ways to laugh at life. I saw that characteristic in Jim more than thirty years ago, and I still love it today."

One has the impression that Shirley could take a week or two to tell you about her husband's attributes. She really believes in her man. And—she worries about him.

"I am concerned about his health and his safety," she says. "He is carrying such a heavy load of responsibility. People are pulling on him all the time. He really needs more time for relaxation and rest. I am also worried about his safety. His efforts to fight hard-core and violent pornography have put him into opposition with an $8 billion industry, and the porno kingpins are not happy about the pressure he puts on them."

She continues, "I believe we are in a spiritual battle and the forces of Satan are against us. I really sensed this when Jim was on the Attorney General's Commission on Pornography. Our children were under such unusual attacks during that period I can only conclude that Satan was harassing us. We almost lost our kids four times during a six-month period. To counteract this, I bathed our children and Jim in prayer. I still spend one day a week fasting and praying for them.

"Jim's ministry was not our idea. It was the Lord's doing. I thought when I married him that he was going to have a full-time psychology practice someday, and later, I thought we would spend our lives in medical research. But the Lord specifically placed Jim in this ministry, and I am depending on Him to sustain us."

When asked to explain the near loss of their children, Shirley tells this story. "One rainy night I was working in the kitchen. Jim had gone pheasant hunting with Ryan in Northern California, and I was home alone. All at once I had a strong urge to pray for Danae. She was a student at USC at the time, and she was out with her boyfriend.

"At first I ignored the impression, but it was so strong that I put down what I was doing and went into the bedroom. There I prayed for Danae's safety, wherever she was and whatever she was doing.

"In a few minutes a policeman knocked on the front door. He told me that Danae had been driving on a winding mountain road above the city. A light rain was falling, and the road was slick from accumulated oil during the long summer months. When mixed with gravel that had washed off the mountain, it became a death trap.

"Danae came around a curve at thirty miles per hour and hit that slick mixture. She lost control of the car and was thrown into the mountain, rolling the car over on its top. Immediately to the left of the road was a five-hundred-foot precipice—a sheer drop-off with no guardrail. No one has gone over that cliff and lived. Danae's car slid on its top to within ten feet of the edge before it stopped.

"As the car rolled, she crushed her left hand, and her friend hurt his neck. Neither of them sustained life-threatening injuries, although Danae had to drop out of college for a semester to have surgery and physiotherapy on her hand."

Shirley concludes, "We feel the Lord urged me to pray that night and then answered my request. As I said, we went through near-death episodes four times during Jim's last six months on the Commission. Why? I can only speculate."

In their early years, the Dobsons followed Dr. Narramore's sage advice and postponed their first baby for five years. Shirley taught school throughout that time so she could help pay Jim's enormous tuition bills at USC. Then they scraped together enough money to buy their first little house for $21,900. It wasn't big, but it was cute and it was theirs. They busily patched and painted and papered and planted every inch of the place. They couldn't afford furniture yet, so they invested in only one important room—the nursery. It soon became apparent that they were going to need it.

Rev. and Mrs. Dobson were invited to their son's house for what they thought was a birthday dinner for Myrtle. At the end of the meal, Shirley brought out a cake bearing the inscription, "Happy Birthday, Grandmother." At first, the subtlety escaped Myrtle. Then she caught it! She jumped to her feet and ran around and around the table, laughing and waving her hands above her head. She and Jim, Sr. had just about given up dreaming for a grandchild since Jim, Jr. was their only hope. He had seemed more interested in books than babies, and the years were flying by. Then suddenly, a little Dobson was in escrow. What a night that was.

Shirley had an uncomplicated pregnancy without a single day of sickness. "No couple was ever better prepared for a baby," she recalls. Unfortunately, they weren't quite as ready as they thought. Halfway through the ninth month, they remembered something they had forgotten. Shirley awakened Jim at 3 A.M. to report the onset of cramping. "Here we go," she warned.

Jim timed the contractions and agreed that Shirley needed to be on her way to the hospital. Then it suddenly dawned on them that they hadn't taken any photographs of Shirley in maternity clothes. She got up, put on her dress, applied her makeup, and posed for Jim's camera in front of the living room fireplace.

There she stood with her little suitcase in hand, ready to run to the hospital. But something strange was not going on inside. The contractions had stopped. The Dobsons went back to bed and waited two more weeks before the baby arrived.

Finally the big day came, and little Danae Ann was born. But all their preparations were wasted. "Everything just blew apart," Shirley recalls. "My mother became sick and couldn't come help me. Then I developed a severe spinal headache and was barely functional myself. Meanwhile, all our friends, who were so anxious for us to join them in parenthood, came calling to see our new baby. We were exhausted from all the company. And poor Jim was up every night with Danae. It was a wild time, despite our careful preparation. Looking back on that period, I think it's rather funny that this family psychologist started his own family in such a state of chaos!"

Like his father, Jim never was too skilled at handling babies, although he was fascinated with his newborn daughter. Shirley still laughs about the Saturday afternoon she went shopping and left Danae in her dad's care. The USC and UCLA football teams were locked in a desperate battle for a Rose Bowl bid, and Jim was terribly excited about the game. Danae chose that time to howl for two hours. The only way he could keep her quiet was to carry her while walking. So Jim strolled in a circle for the entire length of the game, holding his infant daughter to his chest and begging her to go "nite-nite."

"But that wasn't the end of his day," Shirley recalls. "I came home when the stores closed at 6 P.M. and found the nursery light on. I'll never forget what I saw when I opened the door. Jim was changing Danae's diaper, and he had stuffed two large cotton balls in his nose to block the smell. His nostrils were flared from the pressure of the cotton, and he talked with a nasal twang. I stood and laughed at him for ten minutes as he struggled to get the diaper straight."

Shirley continues, "There has never been any doubt, however, about Jim's love for his kids or their great affection for him. I sometimes worry about how they will cope when they lose him. They depend on him so much. Jim began building a secure relationship with Danae and Ryan from their infancies. He put them to bed every night for years and read Dr. Ken Taylor's *Stories for the Children's Hour* to them. In later years he drove the kids to school once a week and told them his own unique adventure stories. This is where the lovable dog Woof was born, who is now the subject of a series of children's books written by Danae. There were four children in the car pool, and they loved his stories about Woof. One day as he told them a story, he decided to let Woof die. It was a big mistake. All four children were bawling as they left the car for class, and that afternoon they promptly demanded that he resurrect the animal. Woof lives on to this day."

When Danae was thirty months old, Shirley decided to serve as a substitute teacher two days a week to provide additional income. On those days, Danae attended a small nursery school near their home. One morning as Jim stopped the car to deposit Danae, she clung to his arms and begged him not to go. Knowing that toddlers never like their parents to leave, he confidently took her to the front door of the school. Then he looked in Danae's eyes and saw she was terrified. This was no routine temper tantrum. He politely told the administrator that his daughter would not be staying that day and took the child back to the car. There he hugged her and said, "Danae, I don't know what has been going on in that school, but you will *never* be left here again." And she wasn't. Jim and Shirley decided they could do without the added income in order for Shirley to stay at home with their little girl. Although James Dobson has recommended the use of corporal punishment by parents and has sometimes been misjudged as a harsh disciplinarian, he is actually tender-hearted with children. Danae and Ryan will attest to that.

To illustrate the relationship he enjoys today with his grown children, Shirley received their permission to reveal what they wrote to their dad last Father's Day. These loving notes were not written for public consumption, of course, but will provide the flavor of their relationship to their dad.

Danae, age twenty-three, wrote:

Dear Dad,

You are the best father that God ever created on this earth. I knew *before* all the fame and glory, at the ripe old age of three, that I had a very special and unique Dad. The world found this out much later. Through the years, I have never doubted your love for me. I've always known that deep in that rusty heart of yours was the kind of love most children only dream of.

You are my father—my special friend—the person I depend on for guidance, among other things. I love you very much.

Danae

P.S. If I could change you—I wouldn't.

Happy Father's Day

Ryan, age eighteen, was less verbal but no less sincere.

Dad. Well, as usual this is a last minute card, but it's not a last minute thought. Dad, I love you more than words can say. I never know how to express that idea right on paper, but I'm doing my best. I am going to miss you so much next year. But I have one last thing to say. I will make you proud. I won't fail you. I promise.

I love you.

Love, *Ryan*

Encased in a small frame in the Dobsons' bedroom is the following Scripture preserved in needlepoint, "I have no greater joy than to hear that my children are walking in the truth" (3 John 1:4 NIV). It is the predominant theme of their home.

That the Dobsons have maintained a protected, private life of their own and with their children is a miracle, of sorts. As the mantle of notoriety settled upon them, they had to learn to cope with an entirely new set of circumstances. The number of people seeking Dr. Dobson's involvement or blessing on their projects has increased exponentially with the passage of time. Everywhere he goes he is handed letters, brochures, and written proposals to be considered. The ministry receives up to 200,000 cards and letters every month, and every one of them is given careful consideration by staff members. None is ignored. Yet the amount of work James Dobson personally can do is limited, and he has learned to recognize and live within these limitations. He has never allowed the world to intrude into his home life, but he has to battle at times to keep it out.

There have been other implications of the Dobsons' visibility in recent years. They are often recognized on the street or in business establishments wherever they go. Dobson sincerely feels honored by these encounters and enjoys talking to people who have been touched by his ministry. Shirley feels that way, too, unless she and Jim have attempted to seclude themselves for a special time together. Even then, the greeter is unlikely to know he or she has intruded on their private lives.

Sometimes the public encounters are humorous. A few years ago, on the Friday before Easter, Jim went to a barber shop for a haircut. The shop was crowded with people who were being entertained, more or less, by three unruly children making nuisances of themselves. They were sassy to their mother, who simply did not have control of the situation. She spoke harshly to the youngest child and sat him down firmly in a chair, only to have him tell her to leave him alone and then return to his antics. This frustrated woman, who has since become a friend of the Dobsons, was exasperated. At that moment she looked up and recognized the psychologist. In a loud voice heard by every patron in the shop, she said, "Oh, Dr. Dobson, I'm so glad to meet you. Why, I've raised all my kids by the principles in your books."

On other occasions Dobson's kids provided the embarrassment. One Sunday night, Dobson spoke in a church in Santa Ana, California, on the subject of discipline. He emphasized the importance of taking charge and being the boss of one's own family. Afterward, people were waiting in line to discuss particular disciplinary problems with him, when he heard a pounding noise coming from the balcony! He looked up in time to see ten-year-old Danae and her five-year-old brother running, fighting, and giggling across the pews in the upper part of the sanctuary. He would have clobbered them if he could have reached them. But then, what would he have said to the people seeking his advice?

I asked Shirley if Jim is still as romantic as he was during college days when he slipped her love notes in her Coke bottle. She acknowledged that he has less time now than when they were young but that his *heart* is still romantically inclined. On their most recent anniversary, for example, he took her on a date that he called "Old Haunts." Beginning in the early afternoon, they revisited some of the places they used to frequent when their relationship was new. They ate at the Italian restaurant in Hollywood where they had enjoyed their first date. They went to Farmer's Market where they had browsed on their fourth anniversary. And finally, they saw a stage play at the Pasadena Playhouse where they had gone on their second date back in 1957.

"It was one of the most wonderful evenings we've ever had together," Shirley recalls.

The most romantic thing Jim ever did occurred some years ago, however. He had been in Boston with his hospital colleagues for two weeks, and he missed Shirley terribly. Ironically, as he sat in his hotel room composing a letter to her, a knock came on the door. He opened it and saw two teenage prostitutes offering him their favors.

71

"No thanks," he said, shutting the door. He went back to writing and asked Shirley to be ready to go to dinner with him when he flew back to Los Angeles. Then he called Shirley's good mother and asked her to be prepared to spend the night with the children, but to make Shirley think they were coming home late.

After Jim and Shirley had gone to dinner and the theater that evening, Jim drove to a beach community where he had made reservations at a good hotel. Shirley didn't catch on until Jim opened her door and invited her to join him.

"But I don't have a toothbrush or anything I need to spend the night," she said with a smile.

"No sweat," said her husband. "We'll buy whatever is required."

"That was the neatest night we ever had," Shirley says. "When he puts his mind to it, Jim can be the most romantic man on earth."

Another romantic highlight of their lives occurred in 1985 when the Dobsons were invited to the White House for a state dinner. "You can't imagine how exciting that was," Shirley says with a twinkle in her eye. "The Marine guards, the beauty of the White House and the East Room at night, the white-gloved butlers who served the meal to us, and of course, having dinner with the president—it was just dazzling. I felt like Cinderella at the ball."

One funny thing happened on that glamorous night. At the last minute Jim said, "Hey, Shirley! We can't go riding up to the White House in a taxi cab." So he called his assistant, Dee Otte, in Los Angeles and asked her to obtain a limo for three hours. Having never rented a luxury car and driver before, she didn't know what to request. As it turned out, Dee secured the longest car in the history of automobiles. The Dobsons then came rolling up to the White House entrance in what seemed like a sixty-foot Cadillac. One of the secret service agents there, Jack Woodward, has since become a personal friend of the Dobsons. He was standing just inside the hallway when he saw the nose of this car begin to pass the doorway. "It went by for half an hour," he laughed.

When it comes to making a family work properly, Shirley is pretty romantic in her own right. Having come from a dysfunctional family, which was dominated by her alcoholic father, she developed a deep longing for stability and harmony at home. Still, years of struggle lay ahead. Shirley's parents were divorced eventually, and her mother, Alma, had to try to support her little family on her own. She worked so hard to meet the needs of her children, but it took every dollar she could earn to feed and clothe them. All through those hard times, Shirley was praying in her bedroom each night, asking the Lord to bring another "father" into their family who would love and care for them. Then, a miracle happened. God brought a wonderful man named Joe Kubishta into their lives. Joe had never been married, and he quickly fell in love with Alma and her two children. He provided the warmth and stability that they needed so desperately. The Kubishtas have now been happily married for thirty-eight years and are serving the Lord in their community.

But Shirley has never forgotten the pain and poverty of her youth. She says today, "When I was a child, it was a big deal if I got a doll for Christmas. We were simply not able to celebrate the holidays in ways that other families enjoyed. The problem was not just a lack of money. I longed for something I couldn't quite describe. Then when I met Jim and he introduced me to his family, I saw what had been missing. It was *tradition*. The Dobsons came from a Southern heritage that was steeped in their own history and in their own unique ways of doing things.

"For example," Shirley says, "I noticed how important the holidays were in the Dobson household. Myrtle made or bought little inexpensive stocking gifts for everyone. She was so creative that it was really fun to receive her surprises. Other women of the family prepared their traditional dishes, such as apple pie and ambrosia. The celebration was played out according to traditions that dated back for decades. Even today, we use Jim's grandmother's china and do things in a way that links us to the past. This became so important to me.

"I know it has become difficult for families to create the traditional flavor I am describing," Shirley continues. "We are all so busy, and it is not easy to add those special touches that make a family feel unique. But I believe it is worth the effort to do it right if circumstances permit. That's why I'm grateful for the role models I had during the early years of our married life."

Shirley went on to develop her own traditions and style. "I believe the home should reflect the feminine touch if possible. That makes it special. It need not be expensive to do that. For the dinner meal, for example, I rarely permit a ketchup bottle or a jar of salad dressing to sit on the table. That's okay for lunch, but the evening meal should have a bit of class to it. I like to use candles quite often and, if they're available, some fresh flowers from the yard. These are the things we couldn't have when I was a child, and I love them today.

"Sometimes we sit near the fireplace and have a romantic dinner in front of a low flame. And on holidays I try to be creative. For example, on Valentine's Day I might choose a red theme. I decorate the table in red, and I give Jim and the kids gifts wrapped in red paper. The meal is red, too! I fix spaghetti with red meat sauce, red Jell-O, and pink cupcakes.

"Please understand that I'm not always successful in giving my home the feeling I'm describing. I have bad days like everyone else when I'm overworked or depressed for one reason or another. There are other times when the house is shattered and a secret visitor would have no hint of the things I'm describing. Let's be realistic. No one pulls off a perfect image at home, behind the front door. But what I've described to you is what I *love* and what I strive to achieve. This is my target.

"I also try to do little things that make Jim feel special," she says. "I once read an article that reported on a survey of a thousand men. This poll showed that the thing men wanted most in their home was tranquillity. I try to create that for my husband.

"Our children used to attack him at the front door when he came home from work because they were so excited to see him. I knew that he was worn out and really needed a moment to rest, so we instituted a little policy. We gave him our hugs and kisses and then let him have a thirty-minute rest period to go through the mail, read the paper, or watch the news.

"That brief period of tranquillity invigorated him. Later on, he was able to put the kids to bed and pray with them. Then he was available to me. Every family has to figure out what works for them and then devote themselves to that plan."

Shirley has discovered that her love of tradition and a stylish family life are shared by many other women with whom she's conversed. She is frequently asked to speak on this topic by ladies who also want to make their homes a unique place of love. During a visit to the home of musicians Bill and Gloria Gaither some years ago, Shirley learned that Gloria held many of the same perspectives and had rich ideas of her own. Their mutual interest led them to write a book together, which they titled *Let's Make a Memory.* They crammed it full of ideas for every holiday, for vacations, for the first day of school, for sick days, etc. The book has now sold over 400,000 copies; obviously, Shirley's "good idea" is appreciated by a host of other women around the world.

As a final commentary on the Dobsons' marital relationship, I would like to share my own observations from working with them here at Focus on the Family. I've had an opportunity to watch them relate to each other both in formal working situations and in times of recreation and entertainment. Shirley serves on the Board of Directors for the ministry on which I sit as an executive. That gives me yet another perspective on their interaction.

Shirley defers to Jim in all leadership matters at Focus on the Family. She is reluctant to speak during Board meetings unless she feels strongly about a particular matter. However, she is certainly no doormat or pushover. Shirley has enormous influence with her husband, but she uses it more in their time at home or on occasions when they are alone.

During one of our Cabinet meetings, it is not unusual for Dobson to say "Shirley thought today's radio broadcast was boring. We need to adjust our approach to that particular topic," or, "Shirley liked the new magazine and hoped we will follow that theme in the future." He always respects her opinions and obviously places significance on her likes and dislikes.

Even though Dr. Dobson is clearly in charge, he and his wife are a team. There's no doubt about that. She brings assets that Jim does not possess, and vice versa. He is continually amazed by Shirley's intuitive sense when important decisions are to be made. "She picks up a whole genre of clues that fly over my head," he says. As an afterthought he adds, "I could never deceive her in any way. She would know it within minutes."

I recall one incident in 1987 when Shirley's discernment was apparent to everyone in leadership at Focus on the Family. The ministry had grown to the point where we desperately needed new facilities. At that time we employed approximately five hundred people, who were located in three cities and housed in seven different buildings. We needed additional space, but land prices in the Arcadia area had skyrocketed. The property across the street from our main headquarters was for sale at forty dollars per square foot, which was far out of reach for us. Furthermore, the available piece of land was too small for our needs.

In the meantime, we had received invitations from several groups across the country who were eager to have our organization headquartered in their cities. These loving supporters often included real estate developers who would sell us all the property we needed for a fraction of the appraised value. They introduced us to contractors who would construct our buildings for cost. We were visited by state government representatives who wanted to attract new employers to their area. They offered to pay the salaries of any new employees we hired during the first year of training. Virtually all the states we considered had a lower tax rate than California.

In the ensuing months, several executives visited such cities as Raleigh, North Carolina; Nashville, Tennessee; Dallas, Texas; Denver, Colorado; Seattle, Washington; and San Diego, California. Every one of these cities offered more community support than we were receiving in Arcadia, a lifestyle more conducive to the traditional values we espoused, and better financial arrangements for acquiring new property.

It appeared we were going to move somewhere; we just had to decide which option was best. Enthusiasm began to swell on the executive staff as we considered the possibility of a move, and just about everyone was excited about it—except Shirley and the 470 staff members who would be left behind.

One Sunday morning while our leadership team was having devotions in a Nashville hotel room, Shirley tried to articulate her reservations. "I just don't feel a peace about the idea of moving," she told the group. "We will lose almost all of our loyal employees if we go, and I think we need to keep seeking the will of the Lord."

When it seemed that Shirley was alone in her feelings,

Jim tried to convey his enthusiasm to her in not-so-subtle ways. Once, when we were touring a very small model home in Raleigh, Jim walked briskly through the house and announced, "Yep. I could be very happy here!" Shirley just grinned and rolled her eyes.

When we visited Seattle to consider it, we had breakfast one morning at the Space Needle restaurant. Jim observed that the floor was rotating ever so slowly in order to give guests a 360-degree view of the skyline. He leaned over to Shirley and said, "Honey, at last, we're moving."

Actually, Jim gave Shirley freedom to veto his decision. He felt that if God were really in this move, He would assure not only him but his wife as well. "Jim has an adventuresome spirit. He was ready to go," Shirley says. "But he felt the decision was so important that we both should have peace about it."

The peaceful assurance came when Shirley lifted all of the conditions on her part and told the Lord she would move anywhere He led her. Not long afterward, her instincts proved to be right after all. A Southern California developer stepped forward and offered Focus on the Family thirteen acres of land and a facility twice the size of all our existing buildings combined. We could move in within six months, and we didn't have to lose a single member of our staff due to the fifteen-mile relocation. The developer took our old buildings in trade and sold us the new facility at his cost. And the land, which had been $40.00 per square foot in Arcadia, was purchased in Pomona for $7.50 per square foot.

Furthermore, a wonderful Mennonite family in Pennsylvania came out and put beautiful oak cabinetry and trim throughout the new building at their cost. The result is a campus in a parklike atmosphere that is beyond our fondest dreams. A new 87,000-square-foot distribution center has been added since then, and the miracle continues. Hundreds of guests come through the facility for a tour each week, leading a local hotel manager to say, "We get more requests for your whereabouts than we do for Disneyland." Without Shirley's influence, Focus on the Family might well be struggling to rebuild its loyal staff today in another city.

Shirley's love and respect for Jim are also profound. "He's an incredible person," she once told me. "He is the most energetic person I know. He doesn't shy away from problems, and he handles an enormous amount of stress so well. When he walks through that door at night, I know he is totally committed to me. He may have spent the afternoon in a heavy counseling situation, but when he comes home, he has shut it off. He has been such a good husband to me and father to Danae and Ryan. But most importantly, he has maintained a high priority on the spiritual values in our home. Early in our marriage he established routines for family devotions, prayer time, and Bible study. As we approach our thirtieth anniversary, I can honestly say I have felt so fortunate to have had the opportunity to be his wife."

Before sending this chapter to the publisher, I asked Jim and Shirley to read it for accuracy and to add their thoughts and comments to this point. In response, Jim wrote this additional statement.

Everything you have written about my relationship with Shirley is true, Rolf, and yet I'm afraid your readers will not see us as we really are. We almost appear to be two perfectly matched saints who have floated on a pink cloud above the real world. The truth of the matter is we have a great marriage because we both *want* it, because we have worked hard to achieve it, and because *God* has blessed our love. But we still experience many of the same struggles that others deal with. We fuss at each other when we get fatigued, and we occasionally grate on one another's nerves. We are both capable of being selfish or demanding in times of unusual stress. Our children went through the typical struggles during their adolescent years, and there have been occasions when the pressures of living have made it difficult to breathe. So please make sure your readers understand that we are like other families, and we don't want to be presented as something we're not and can never be.

On the other hand, it is true that Shirley and I are absolutely committed to each other. We find our greatest joy in one another and usually begin our prayer time with thankfulness to God for what He has given us. We love our children and they love us. They are not perfect kids, but they are off to a good start in life. And we are happy people.

Most importantly, please make it clear that we *have* nothing and we *are* nothing without Jesus Christ. He is our hope. He is our salvation. He is the reason for the joy that lies within us. Point not to Jim and

Shirley Dobson, but to the Lord they are humbly attempting to serve as fellow pilgrims in this journey through life.

Dr. Dobson's concern is well taken. Still, in this day of disintegrating marriages and troubled homes, it is healthy, I feel, to have role models to emulate—even if they are imperfect ones. Toward that end, I think it would be inspirational to conclude this chapter by reprinting Jim's eloquent tribute to Shirley and the life they have shared, written during a Marriage Encounter seminar they attended a few years ago.

The beauty of Marriage Encounter is that it has the ability to *float* to wherever the need is greatest. In our case, the need had little to do with communication in the classic sense. Instead, we discovered a secret source of tension that Shirley had not verbalized and I didn't know existed. It had to do with the recent deaths of eight senior members of our small family, six of whom were males. My wife had watched as the survivors struggled to cope with life alone and the awesome implications of sudden widowhood. Because Shirley and I are now in our midforties, she was quietly worrying about the possibility of losing me—and wanting to know where we are going from here. My loving wife was also saying to herself, "I know Jim needed me when we were younger and he was struggling to establish himself professionally. But do I *still* have a prominent place in his heart?"

One simply does not sit down to discuss such delicate matters, voice to voice, in the rush and hubbub of everyday life. They are held inside until (and if) an opportunity to express them is provided. For Shirley and me, that occurred throughout the Marriage Encounter program. In the early part of the weekend, we worked through the possibility of my death. Then on the final morning, the issue of my continued love for her was laid to rest.

Shirley was alone in our hotel room, expressing her private concern in a written statement to me. And by divine leadership I'm sure, I was in another room addressing the same issue even though we had not discussed it. When we came together and renewed our commitment for the future, whatever it might hold, Shirley and I experienced one of the most emotional moments of our lives. It was a highlight of our twenty-one years together, and neither of us will ever forget it.

Although it will require me to share an intensely personal statement between my wife and me, I would like to conclude with a portion of the letter I wrote to her on that memorable morning. I will skip the more intimate details, quoting only the memories that "bonded" me to my bride.

Who else shares the memory of my youth during which the foundations of love were laid? I ask you, who else could occupy the place that is reserved for the only woman who was *there* when I graduated from college and went to the army and returned as a student at USC and bought my first decent car (and promptly wrecked it) and picked out an inexpensive wedding ring with you (and paid for it with Savings Bonds) and we prayed and thanked God for what we had. Then we said the wedding vows and my dad prayed, "Lord, You gave us Jimmy and Shirley as infants to love and cherish and raise for a season, and tonight, we give them back to you after our labor of love—not as two separate individuals, but as one!" And everyone cried.

Then we left for the honeymoon and spent all our money and came home to an apartment full of rice and a bell on the bed, and we had only just begun. You taught the second grade and I taught (and fell in love with) a bunch of sixth graders and especially a kid named Norbert and I earned a master's degree and passed the comprehensive exams for a doctorate and we bought our first little home and remodeled it and I dug up all the grass and buried it in a 10-foot hole which later sank and looked like two graves in the front yard—and while spreading the dirt to make a new lawn, I accidentally "planted" eight million ash seeds from our tree and discovered two weeks later that we had a forest growing between our house and the street.

Then alas, you delivered our very own baby and we loved her half to death and named her Danae Ann and built a room on our little bungalow and gradually filled it with furniture. Then I joined the staff of Children's Hospital and I did well there, but still didn't have enough money to pay our USC tuition and other expenses so we sold (and ate) a Volkswagen. Then I earned a Ph.D. and we cried and thanked God for what we had. In 1970, we brought home a little boy and named him James Ryan and loved him half to death and didn't sleep for six months. And I labored over a manuscript titled "Dare To," something or other and then reeled backward under a flood of favorable responses and a few not so favorable responses and received a small royalty check and thought it was a fortune and I joined the faculty at USC School of Medicine and did well there.

Soon I found myself pacing the halls of Huntington Memorial Hospital as a team of grim faced neurologists examined your nervous system for evidence of hypothalamic tumor and I prayed and begged God to let me complete my life with my best friend, and He finally said, "Yes—for now," and we cried and thanked Him for what we had. And we bought a new house and promptly tore it to shreds and went skiing in Vail, Colorado, and tore your leg to shreds and I called your mom to report the accident and she tore me to shreds and our toddler, Ryan, tore the whole town of Arcadia to shreds. And the construction on the house seemed to go on forever and you stood in the shattered living room and cried every Saturday night because so little had been accomplished. Then during the worst of the mess, 100 friends gave us a surprise housewarming and they slopped through the debris and mud and sawdust and cereal bowls and sandwich parts—and the next morning you groaned and asked, "Did it really happen?"

And I published a new book called *Hide or Seek* (What?) and everyone called it Hide *and* Seek and the publisher sent us to Hawaii and we stood on the balcony overlooking the bay and thanked God for what we had. And I published *What Wives Wish* and people liked it and the honors rolled in and the speaking requests arrived by the hundreds.

Then you underwent risky surgery and I said, "Lord, not now!" And the doctor said, "No cancer!" and we cried and thanked God for what we had. Then I started a radio program and took a leave of absence from Children's Hospital and opened a little office in Arcadia called Focus on the Family, which a three-year-old radio listener later called "Poke us in the Family," and we got more visible.

Then we went to Kansas City for a family vacation and my dad prayed on the last day and said, "Lord, we know it can't always be the wonderful way it is now, but we thank You for the love we enjoy today." A month later he experienced his heart attack and in December I said good-bye to my gentle friend and you put your arm around me and said, "I'm hurting with you!" and I cried and said "I love you!" And we invited my mother to spend six weeks with us during her recuperation period and the three of us endured the loneliest Christmas of our lives as the empty chair and missing place setting reminded us of his red sweater and dominoes and apples and a stack of sophisticated books and a little dog named Benji who always sat on his lap. But life went on. My mother staggered to get herself back together and couldn't and lost fifteen pounds and moved to California and still ached for her missing friend.

And more books were written and more honors arrived and we became better known and our influence spread and we thanked

God for what we had. And our daughter went into adolescence and this great authority on children knew he was inadequate and found himself asking God to help him with the awesome task of parenting and He did and we thanked Him for sharing His wisdom with us.

And then a little dog named Siggie who was sort of a dachshund grew old and toothless and we had to let the vet do his thing, and a fifteen-year-love affair between man and dog ended with a whimper. But a pup named Mindy showed up at the front door and life went on. Then a series of films were produced in San Antonio, Texas, and our world turned upside down as we were thrust into the fishbowl and "Poke us in the Family" expanded in new directions and life got busier and more hectic and time became more precious and then someone invited us to a Marriage Encounter weekend where I sit at this moment.

So I ask you! Who's gonna take your place in my life? You have become me and I have become you. We are inseparable. I've now spent 46 percent of my life with you, and I can't even remember much of the first 54! Not one of the experiences I've listed can be comprehended by anyone but the woman who lived through them with me. Those days are gone, but their aroma lingers on in our minds. And with every event during these twenty-one years, our lives have become more intertwined—blending eventually into this incredible affection that I bear for you today.

Is it any wonder that I can read your face like a book when we are in a crowd? The slightest narrowing of your eyes speaks volumes to me about the thoughts that are running through your conscious experience. As you open Christmas presents, I know instantly if you like the color or style of the gift, because your feelings cannot be hidden from me.

I love you, S.M.D. (remember the monogrammed shirt)? I love the girl who believed in me before I believed in myself. I love the girl who never complained about huge school bills and books and hot apartments and rented junky furniture and no vacations and humble little Volkswagens. You have been *with* me—encouraging me, loving me, and supporting me since August 27, 1960. And the status you have given me in our home is beyond what I have deserved.

So why do I want to go on living? It's because I have you to take that journey with. Otherwise, why make the trip? The half life that lies ahead promises to be tougher than the years behind us. It is in the nature of things that my mom will someday join my father and then she will be laid to rest beside him in Olathe, Kansas, overlooking a wind-swept hill from whence he walked with Benji and recorded a cassette tape for me describing the beauty of that spot. Then we'll have to say good-bye to your Mom and Dad. Gone will be the table games we played and the Ping Pong and lawn darts and Joe's laughter and Alma's wonderful ham dinners and her underlined birthday cards and the little yellow house in Long Beach. Everything within me screams "No!" But my Dad's final prayer is still valid—"We know it can't always be the way it is now." When that time comes, our childhoods will then be severed—cut off by the passing of the beloved parents who bore us.

What then, my sweet wife? To whom will I turn for solace and comfort? To whom can I say, "I'm hurting!" and know that I am understood in more than an abstract manner? To whom can I turn when the summer leaves begin to change colors and fall to the ground? How much I have enjoyed the springtime and the warmth of the summer sun. The flowers and the green grass and the blue sky and the clear streams have been savored to their fullest. But alas, autumn is coming. Even now, I can feel a little nip in the air—and I try not to look at a distant, lone cloud that passes near the horizon. I must face the fact that winter lies ahead—with its ice and sleet and snow to pierce us through. But in this instance, winter will not be followed by springtime, except in the glory of the life to come. With whom, then, will I spend that final season of my life?

None but you, Shirls. The only joy of the future will be in experiencing it as we have the past twenty-one years—hand in hand with the one I love . . . a young miss named Shirley Deere, who gave me everything she had—including her heart.

Thank you, babe, for making this journey with me. Let's finish it—together!

Your Jim

That is known as marital bonding!

6

Life in the Fast Lane

Shirley Dobson stood by her husband during the sweat and grime of a seven-year-long graduate program. She never complained but simply resigned herself to the postponement of what she called the "real" world. It would come in time, she knew. But she did have her limit, and the Dobsons ran into it near the end of 1966. Unbelievably to her, just as Jim was closing in on his final academic requirements for his Ph.D., he began talking about a new goal. He wanted to go to medical school. They had dreamed about the day he would finish his degree and escape from the educational pressures that had dominated their lives. They might even get to take vacations someday like normal people and spend their weekends working in the yard or shopping for furniture. But now as the end was virtually in sight, Jim came up with this crazy idea to start over with five tough years to go. And of course, Shirley knew they would be in debt a mile deep by the time he earned his M.D. What then? Would he specialize? How many *more* years would be taken from them? Thinking about it was enough to send her running down the road, screaming.

Shirley didn't scream, and she didn't run, but she did let Jim know how strongly she felt about his idea. Beyond that, she found a way to work off her frustration. Jim noticed that every time he talked about going to medical school, Shirley went outside and raked leaves to vent her anxieties.

"Whenever I needed yardwork done, I just brought up the subject of further schooling," Jim now says in jest.

Dobson went so far as to investigate the possibility of enrolling in the USC School of Medicine as soon as he had finished his final oral examinations for the Ph.D. He was told that he would be welcomed as a continuing student there. However, after considering all the ramifications for his wife and daughter (who was a toddler at the time), Jim wisely decided to drop the notion altogether. The price was simply too great at that late date. Ironically, a few months after he gave up his ambition, he was invited to join the medical staff for Children's Hospital of Los Angeles, and three years later, he became a member of the faculty of USC School of Medicine. He held the academic rank of assistant professor of pediatrics initially and later, associate clinical professor of pediatrics. Thus, instead of being a student at the prestigious institutions, he became a member of the professional staff and faculty for both.

During Dr. Dobson's subsequent seventeen years at Children's Hospital and fourteen years at USC (served concurrently), he was first assigned to the Division of Child Development and later the Division of Medical Genetics, where he conducted research on children with various metabolic disorders leading to mental retardation. Principal among these investigations was the "Collaborative Study of Children Treated for Phenylketonuria," which was conducted in fifteen major medical centers across the United States. Dr. Dobson directed this $5 million, fifteen-year project, which involved the work of more than 250 doctors and professionals in seven disciplines. His responsibility required him to help design the study and then visit the medical centers regularly to coordinate the effort. The findings from that study now determine the way phenylketonuric children are treated, and reports of it can be found in the current medical textbooks.

Those were absolutely wonderful years for Dobson, whose work allowed him to explore the fascinating relationship between intellectual development and medicine. He wrote a number of scientific articles that were published in the most prestigious medical journals of the time, including the *New England Journal of Medicine, Lancet* (an English publication),

Pediatrics, and the *Journal of Pediatrics.* He also coedited with Dr. Richard Koch a graduate textbook entitled *The Mentally Retarded Child and His Family.* It was recognized as a groundbreaking work. In fact, the highly respected Menninger Clinic recommended this text to health professionals with this endorsement: "If you can only have one book on your shelf about mental retardation, this should be it."

At the same time that this world of medical research was expanding for Dr. Dobson, another career as a family psychologist was forming beneath him. Fortunately, he was given time to pursue it. Members of the medical staff at Children's Hospital were only required to work four days per week, providing the fifth day for private practice or other professional activities. Dr. Dobson used his time for counseling, speaking, and writing. To his surprise, this "other world" expanded as rapidly for him as the primary responsibility at the hospital. Looking back, it is clear that he reached the point of professional preparation at a time when the need for his expertise was at an all-time high.

Who can forget what was going on in the United States and around the world in the late 1960s? Social upheaval reigned supreme, especially for those young people just then reaching college age. Specifically addressing the high school class that graduated in 1965, Dobson spoke of them as a "lost" generation in perhaps the most tragic and unstable era in American history. This is the way he described them in his book *The Strong-Willed Child*:

A few weeks after this class received their diplomas, our cities began to burn during the long hot summer of racial strife. That signaled the start of the chaos to come. They entered college at a time when drug abuse was not only prevalent, but became almost universal for students and teachers alike. Intellectual deterioration was inevitable in this narcotic climate. The Viet Nam War soon heated campus passions to an incendiary level, generating anger and disdain for the government, the President, the military, both political parties, and indeed, the American way of life. That hostility gave rise to bombings and riotings and burning of "establishment" edifices. This generation of college students had already witnessed the brutal assassination of their romantic idol, John F. Kennedy, when they were barely sixteen years old. Then at a critical point in their season of passion they lost two more beloved heroes, Robert Kennedy and Martin Luther King. Those murders were followed by the killing of students at Kent State University and the street wars that punctuated the 1968 Democratic Convention. These violent convulsions reached their overt culmination in the wake of President Nixon's military foray into Cambodia, which virtually closed down American campuses.

Accompanying this social upheaval was a sudden disintegration of moral and ethical principles, such as has never occurred in the history of mankind. All at once, there were no definite values. There were no standards. No absolutes. No rules. No traditional beliefs on which to lean. Nor could anyone over thirty even be trusted. And as will be recalled, some bright-eyed theologians chose that moment of confusion to announce the death of God. It was a distressing time to be so young—to be groping aimlessly in search of personal identity and a place in the sun.

For a while, it looked like the entire nation was going to hell in a handbasket. Parents were confused by permissive childrearing techniques. Some mainline churches rearranged their code of ethics, permitting homosexual liaisons and extramarital affairs under the banner of Christianity. Many public schools became armed camps and seemed to forget why students were sent there. Flower children shared hypodermic needles and spread venereal diseases to one another, while their parents tried vainly to find them. Open marriage and wife swapping became the rage. It was, in the opinion of many, a time of national disgrace and unprecedented social upheaval.

It was at this precise moment of turbulence that James Dobson entered the prime of his professional life. At thirty-one years of age and armed with a rock-solid system of values cultivated from his childhood, he began to call the nation back to traditional understandings. He stood virtually alone for a period of time, although people listened when he spoke. His voice had a ring of authority to it. He condemned the so-called new morality, he demanded more discipline in the schools, he taught parents how to reassert their authority at home, and he unflinchingly called sin by its biblical name—*Sin*! The response was incredible. It was as though the Christian community and even many nonbelievers had been waiting for someone to say what they

87

already knew to be true, and they opened their doors and their hearts to this young psychologist.

Even so, Dobson's speaking career began ever so humbly. He accepted every opportunity to share his views that came his way—from PTA chapters, groups of parents in homes, Bible study associations, Sunday school classes, and teacher conferences. In the early days, Dobson's speaking skills were less than polished, and he knew it. So he was always extremely well-prepared in order to maximize his effectiveness. Gradually, he developed a style with which he could be comfortable.

Very early in his career, however, before that state of competence had been achieved, Dr. Dobson was asked to speak at a prominent Japanese church in Los Angeles. It was a serious challenge for him so soon after graduating from USC. To ease his nervousness, he prepared for weeks in anticipation of the big night. Unfortunately, he got lost on the way to the church and arrived late and out of breath. He ran into the sanctuary where the "congregation" waited, and as he walked down the aisle to the front, he noticed there were no adults in the audience. The church was filled with junior high students who had been invited to hear the psychologist speak. In his hands were carefully outlined notes for an address to a grown-up audience on the subject of discipline.

Dobson turned and looked into the faces of three hundred expectant kids, to whom he had *nothing* to say. Panic gripped his heart, and he developed his first case of "flop sweat." Every entertainer or speaker knows what that experience is like—when the blood pressure rises in response to failure, and sweat begins to run down the forehead and neck.

Dobson began pulling stuff out of the air to try to interest those kids. He says today, "Who knows what in the world I told them that night?"

But everyone has to start somewhere, and these humble beginnings were not to last long. Within a few years, he was making guest appearances on the nationally syndicated "Dinah Shore Show," Tom Snyder's "Tomorrow Show," "AM America," Barbara Walters' "Not for Women Only," and many others. Hundreds of speaking invitations that couldn't be accepted rolled in. And, he was still involved full-time at USC and Children's Hospital. There *had* to be a better way to get the message out.

In late 1970 on a Sunday afternoon, Shirley and Jim received a telephone call from the social chairman of their church fellowship. She had an assignment for them. "There was a couple in our service this morning named Francis and Joyce Heatherly," she said. "No one knows much about them, but we would like to make them feel welcome in our church. Would you invite them to your house after the service tonight?"

The Dobsons had planned to take a nap that afternoon, but they agreed to entertain this new couple. That meant they had to straighten the house, go to the store, and prepare to receive the guests. The Heatherlys did indeed come for a visit, and the two couples quickly struck up a friendship. Midway through the evening, Francis asked Jim what his future plans were.

"Well, I've been speaking quite a bit on the subject of child rearing," he said. "I find that people are so hungry for basic information, not only about handling kids, but about what is going on in the world around us."

What Dr. Dobson didn't know was that Francis had been director of marketing for one of the largest Christian publishing companies in the United States. The next day, representatives from Word, Tyndale House, and Zondervan called him at the hospital. Two of the three companies, Tyndale and Zondervan, immediately offered generous contracts for a yet-to-be-written book, and six months later *Dare to Discipline* was in print.

Dr. and Mrs. Dobson requested 250 copies of their newly published book to send to influential people and to his professional colleagues. Jim personally autographed all the books, and then together, he and Shirley laboriously packaged them, addressed the envelopes, stamped them all, and wrote, "Special Fourth Class Mail, Book" 250 times on the labels. There in the family room of their first little house, they then got down on their knees and laid their hands on the pile of books. Jim prayed a prayer of dedication, asking God to bless his labor in the work of the kingdom. Finally, they carefully carried the packages to his Volkswagen and headed for the post office.

The response was immediate—and overwhelming. Tyndale's

marketing director, Bob Hawkins (who suggested the title for the book), telephoned Dobson one night at home. "Do you know what is about to happen to your life?" he asked.

"Not really," Dobson said. "Tell me."

What happened was that the psychologist's world turned upside down. *Dare to Discipline* was a best seller, and the mantle of notoriety mentioned earlier began to descend upon the author and his family. Even today, some twenty years later, *Dare to Discipline* still ranks as one of the top twenty Christian best sellers in the United States. Though it is out of date and bears the flavor of the Vietnam War and that troubled era, the book still appeals to those who know that the values we abandoned as a nation during that historic period are still valid and must be readopted if we are to survive as a people.

One of his closest friends at Children's Hospital, Dr. Malcolm Williamson, predicted to Dobson in 1971 that *Dare to Discipline* would sell two million copies. It was an audacious expectation to be sure, but it proved accurate. To understand the significance of this success, one must realize that hundreds of thousands of manuscripts are written by aspiring authors and submitted to publishers every year. Of these, approximately 50,000 are selected for publication and make it to the bookstore. The average title sells fewer than 10,000 copies, and a best seller is considered to be any book that is purchased by 50,000 readers. In recognition of its contribution to society, *Dare to Discipline* was selected in 1972 to be specially bound and placed in the White House library.

In short, James Dobson's arrival on the scene coincided exactly with a revolutionary social movement that shook America to its foundations. He was God's man for that hour, and he was ready for the assignment.

Not everyone was wildly enthusiastic about Dobson's emphasis on firm and loving discipline, of course. After receiving a well-earned spanking, one three-year-old girl threw her mother's copy of *Dare to Discipline* in the toilet. Dr. Dobson also received a letter from an irritated seven-year-old girl who had just had her seat warmed by her father. These are her exact words:

Dear Dobonson:

You are a mean and curle thing. You and your dumb sayings whon't take you to heaven. Kids don't like wippens.

Kristy

Dr. Benjamin Spock may have been loved by children who were raised by his permissive parenting philosophies, but Dr. Dobson had a whole generation of kids who wanted to catch him in a blind alley. Nevertheless, he continued to write best-selling books, including *Hide or Seek* in 1974 (about building self-esteem in children), *What Wives Wish Their Husbands Knew About Women* in 1975 (dealing with sources of depression in women), *The Strong-Willed Child* in 1978 (which helped parents cope with assertive offspring), and *Preparing for Adolescence* in 1978 (directed to children on the threshold of the teen years). All these books are still in print, and most continue to be best sellers.

It is easy to understand the pressure cooker that James Dobson was creating at this point in his life. His positions at Children's Hospital and the medical school were demanding and exciting, yet this other world of family psychology could hardly be ignored. The man who spoke so often about reserving time for one's spouse and children was in danger of losing his. And Sunday offered no respite. He could hardly attend his own church without being approached by some friend who needed advice about parenting or marriage. Week after week, the Dobson automobile was usually the last one to drive out of the parking lot.

During this time Shirley was complaining to Jim about his hectic schedule, of course. He knew she was right and hated the pace at which he ran, but he honestly didn't know what to do about it. He has never been a classic workaholic—one who is neurotically addicted to work and is happy only when he is on the job. That doesn't fit Jim's personality. He loves being with his wife and kids, likes to read, ski, watch college and professional sports, and, especially, play basketball. He plays "roundball" two hours per day, three times each week—even today at fifty-three! No, he was not overcommitted by design. He just couldn't figure out how to do what he thought he should.

One characteristic with which Dobson has had to deal has been his "tremendous capacity for work." That was the observation of the pediatrician with whom he served at Children's Hospital. All of us who hold positions of senior leadership at Focus understand that comment and are well acquainted with Dobson's remarkable productivity. In working with him, a person can clearly see how he has been able in one lifetime to teach at all levels from elementary through graduate and medical schools, write eleven best-selling books, counsel those in need, produce several highly acclaimed films, host fifteen hundred daily radio programs, serve three presidents of the United States, speak periodically for twenty years, consult with the Pentagon, teach a Sunday school class, and in his spare time build a fifty-million-dollar, nonprofit ministry. And, except for short periods early in his career, he has done this without neglecting his family. How was this possible? By not wasting a moment of his fifty-three years. His college friend, Jim Davis, summed up this characteristic of Dobson by saying, "He is incredibly productive and a voracious reader. That enables him to do everything so quickly."

Still, there was a period when Dobson's two careers were booming simultaneously and he began to neglect his family. He *knew* better because the people he loved were urging him to straighten out his priorities. True to form, his father said it best. He had seen the crisis coming several years before, and he was concerned about this side of his son's temperament. As he and Myrtle were going to Hawaii that August, he used those five uninterrupted hours on the airplane to write a historic letter to Jim, Jr. These rather formal words carried the impact of a sledge hammer for the busy son who received them.

Dear Jimbo,

It's been some time since I wrote you a fatherly letter, or any letters of any kind. It is worthy of note, I think, that of all the scores of communications that go to make up our total correspondence, including those of your high school and college days, I can recall no letter that had to be written in anger or even a mild reprimand, and none from this vantage point, that is not accompanied by a nostalgic aura of pleasantness. In a word, today I feel more like saying that it has been great to be your father—though the success of the relationship, on mature reflection, seems far more the result of your relation to me rather than any excellence on my part. I am proud to be a member of the team.

My prayer and hope and expectation is that the same reverential affinity under God will always exist between you and your children. I am very sure that love and faith in a living Christ are always the only cornerstones, the only building blocks for the making of memories that bless rather than burn. I'm very happy about your success, which is now coming in like showers. It is important for men, in all vocations, to experience the realization of their dreams. At this point, you have had a very high ratio of positive returns on your endeavors—almost unbelievable, in fact.

I don't need to remind you that it won't always be so. Life will test you deeply, if only in the ultimate when we have to lay down everything. To this point, you have been largely untested, but trials are inevitable. If frustration and heartbreak do not come relative to your career, you must mentally prepare for it in some other areas. I know this is largely impossible to do in a day of sunshine and roses, "sufficient unto the day is the evil thereof," but we should also add "only for those who keep a stronghold on God through the happy times."

We must all pray definitely, pointedly and continuously for your children. They are growing up in the wickedest section of a world much farther gone into moral decline than the world into which you were born. I have observed that one of the greatest delusions is to suppose that children will be devout Christians simply because their parents have been, or that any of them will enter into life in any other way than through the valley of deep travail of prayer and faith. Failure at this point, for you, would make mere success in business a very pale and washed-out affair indeed. But this prayer demands time, time that cannot be given if it is all signed and conscripted and laid on the altar of career ambition.

In my case, there was a happy coincidence of my career as a minister with the care of your soul, and I'm without regret that the modest appointments which were mine to fill in your childhood offered me the time to pray for you. In your case, it will have to be done by design—jealously guarded, conscious design. The future—all the future—is ultimately all brightness for any Christian, and today mine looks particularly bright. But the tragedy of a child who has made shipwreck of faith in life can mar the old age of anyone, Christian or otherwise. We must all work together to achieve for you the serenity which is mine in this respect, as I enter the youth of my old age. That is only one more reason we should all drink to the full the cup that is still in our hands.

Love, your Dad

Jim buckled under the convicting power of his father's words. He saw clearly what his dad was trying to tell him. All the success in the world would mean nothing if he did not get to know his son and daughter and failed to lead them to Christ.

Still, there was no easy solution to the problem. In the meantime he was spanning two, divergent fields that were growing further and further apart. He could not even keep up with the literature in each profession. During that period, Dobson was like the old film character who had one foot on the dock and the other on the boat. It was only a matter of time until he lost his footing in both and plunged into the water.

Obviously, there was only one thing to do. He would have to abandon one of the two careers. But which one? His position at Children's Hospital was a coveted assignment that men and women worked years to achieve. He was happy there. He was well respected there. He felt fulfilled in the hospital environment. He was helping prevent mental retardation in children, and he loved kids.

On the other hand, the institution of the family was unraveling, and he felt he could help. There wasn't much time left. Every day, the values in which he believed seemed to be ebbing away. He knew he had workable answers to many of the nation's problems, not because they were based on his own concepts or the faddish ideas of the times, but because they were rooted in these eternal truths: the permanence of marriage, the value of bearing and raising children, the balance between love and discipline, the dignity of the human spirit, and the worth of even the most insignificant individual on earth, including the unwanted, preborn child. These ideas were based on immutable truths that would stand the test of time. Should he throw caution to the wind and devote the rest of his life to their propagation?

He contemplated this tough decision for more than two years. Ultimately, Dobson felt that God was calling him to serve the families who sought his help. He took a one-year leave of absence from the hospital (he resigned the following year) and opened a little two-office suite in Arcadia, California. It was not much of a beginning. He had left a thriving medical center with a large staff under him and the participation of hundreds of professionals from across the country. Behind him was an accounting department, a legal department, a bevy of physicians, and one of the best universities in America. Instead, he now rode his bicycle each day to his quiet little office and wondered if the phone would ever ring again.

One of the first items of business was to get organized legally. Jim and Shirley appointed an independent board to direct their efforts and assembled them in his office. None of them had any idea about what to expect of their efforts. Peb Jackson, who now serves as senior vice-president for Focus, was among them. He remembers those times with amusement.

The early meetings of the Focus Board dealt with concepts that are unrelated to what the ministry is doing today. None of us held that vision. Here is why we incorporated as a nonprofit organization. Dobson's seminars were drawing 2,000 to 3,000 people per weekend, who each paid about $12 for tickets. Thus, $24,000 to $36,000 was generated at each of these events, less expenses. Dobson didn't feel it was right to accept that huge income for himself, and we wanted to funnel the extra money to other ministries. That was the extent of our foresight. We didn't even know what to call this new organization, so we finally settled on the same name Jim was using for his seminars: Focus on the Family. I wish I could say today that we had a long-range plan for the ministry, but all we wanted to do was get Jim's weekend seminars on a nonprofit footing.

Before long, Dobson began to realize that leaving the hospital and eliminating one of his careers was not sufficient. Travel and speaking were the killers. That's what took him away from his family. His citywide seminars, designed to help him speak to larger crowds in the same amount of time on the road, proved to be exhausting. He would address the attendees for three hours on Friday night and then stand before them all day Saturday. He remained on duty during break times and even after the seminars were over, counseling briefly with hundreds of people who gathered around him. The lunch and dinner periods were usually devoted to someone with a need. Then when the Saturday seminar finally concluded and his strength was gone, the person volunteering to take him to the airport would invariably say something like, "Dr. Dobson, we have this eight-year-old boy, and he has a problem . . . "

Dobson would then fly back to Los Angeles, changing time zones and arriving in the parking lot of Los Angeles International Airport almost too tired to drive home. Shirley could tell from the sound of his footsteps coming up their walkway that he was drained of every reserve. It would take several days for him to recover from these weekend seminars. Something had to be done.

One evening in the spring of 1977, as the Dobsons prayed for a solution, Jim stumbled onto a passage of Scripture in the eighteenth chapter of Exodus that spoke directly to him. In that Old Testament story, Moses was exhausted from working too hard so his father-in-law, Jethro, came to see him. Jethro told him he simply had to get some help. In the final verse of that passage, The Living Bible reads, "If you follow this advice, and if the Lord agrees, there will be peace and harmony in the camp" (Exod. 18:23).

Dobson needed peace and harmony in the camp. The next day he met with his agent, Mac McQuiston, and canceled all but two of his speaking engagements for the next year. Mac was shocked and sat speechless for some time.

"For Pete's sake, Mac. Say *something*!" Dobson finally said.

"I'm just stunned," Mac replied. He knew Jim's decision would topple his young agency. "But if that's what God wants you to do, of course you must do it."

Jim said precisely these words, "Mac, I know that God never works on half an equation. If He's instructing me to do this, and I know He is, then He has something for you on the other side."

He did, indeed. Shortly thereafter, Mac joined Dobson's new organization as executive vice-president, and the two served side by side for years.

That still left a major question unanswered, however. James Dobson had resigned from Children's Hospital in order to reach out to beleaguered families around the country, but the needs of his personal life had just led him to quit speaking. How was he going to get the message out while staying at home?

God had two unbelievable answers waiting in the wings. First, since Jim had canceled his speaking responsibilities for 1978, Francis Heatherly came and suggested that Word Publishing videotape one of the final two seminars.

Dobson thought it was a bad idea. "I don't believe people will sit for seven hours and watch one man speaking on a screen," he told five members of the Word team who had flown to his home to persuade him. He was also wary of the incredible expense of the taping.

"This video project will cost a fortune, and I don't want your blood on my hands," he said. Since a "talking head" series had never been produced for the church market, his publishers were more uncertain of the risks than they let on. They weren't sure if pastors would be willing to devote seven Sunday night services to a series of practical films on family living. They weren't the only ones who had doubts. The respected president of a large advertising/public relations agency had considered the project and concluded that it would not succeed.

But if Dobson's publishers were not convinced in their minds that the project could be successful, they were resolved in their hearts that it needed to be done. When the meeting concluded, the Word executives had convinced him to allow them to bring cameras and equipment to his next-to-last seminar in San Antonio, Texas. The rest is history, as they say.

By today's technical standards, the Focus on the Family film series is amateurish. Word's vice-president in charge of the project, Joey Paul, said only three cameras were used, and their images were recorded on a single video track and were spontaneously chosen by the director. This meant that the seminar was basically recorded like a live event with no options to reedit and splice different angles together in the postproduction process. The sound and the lighting technology were also primitive.

However, these technical problems didn't stand in the way of the films' success. They became an overnight sensation among churches. Like his books, Dobson's films offered "how-to" advice that met real needs, and pastors found that the series helped to swell church attendance.

Word estimates that sixty million people have seen the films to this date—all this while James Dobson has stayed at home with his family. The night he decided to quit traveling, it appeared his speaking ministry to families was over. Yet, by putting his seminar on film, Dobson was able to reach far more families than he ever would have done on the road. And it all started with Exodus 18 and the advice of Moses' long-gone father-in-law. Even today, Dobson accepts virtually none of the two thousand speaking requests which come to him each year. "I can only keep my boat upright if I don't travel," he says.

So much for the themes Dobson was addressing in 1978. But what about the ongoing needs of families across the nation? Did God also have an answer to that dilemma? As a matter of fact, He did.

In 1976 James Dobson began to feel that he should start a radio program. But how could it be supported?

"I only had one thing to bargain with, and that was my writings," he said. "So I boldly began talking to publishers about helping me get on the air. I offered to give my new book to anyone who would donate $35,000 to our new nonprofit ministry, Focus on the Family. Their eyes would glass over immediately, and the conversation would soon terminate."

Finally, Jim asked his good friends at Tyndale if they would accept the offer. After taking several months to think about the proposal, they agreed to help. Dobson then set about writing *The Strong-Willed Child* for them, which has now sold one million copies, and Dr. Taylor wrote a check for $35,000 to a little outfit called Focus on the Family. That permitted Dobson to purchase airtime for the first year of broadcasting, with his program airing once a week on forty-three stations.

When the second year rolled around, Tyndale understandably bowed out. "We've fulfilled our obligation," Dr. Taylor said, and Dobson agreed. However, the projected expenses for the coming year were $60,000. Where would the money come from? If he went ahead with the program, Dobson had to guarantee the payment personally. He wavered momentarily and almost pulled out. Then finally he said, "Let's go." By the end of that year, his listeners were carrying the largest part of the financial load, and the ministry was on its way.

Jim's challenge to his publishers to help Focus has become familiar to those who want to do business with him. He is more concerned about the well-being of the ministry than his personal bank account.

I can remember one instance in 1982 when Dobson was meeting with publishers who were pitching him. They had made an impressive presentation, talking about marketing plans and the strength of their company. They capped their proposal with a generous offer of a large advance and high royalties. I'll never forget Dobson's response. After listening to their entire presentation, he leaned forward in his chair and said, "Fellows, I appreciate everything you have planned for me and my next book. But that's not the point. I'm really not concerned about what you are going to do for me. Tell me what you are going to do for Focus."

From another perspective, Focus didn't seem to need the publishers' help for the next few years. It doubled in size annually. Every index of growth has accelerated on a forty-five-degree angle since its inception. The greatest problem has been managing the expansion so as not to turn over the boat. There are now five radio broadcasts heard throughout the week. The original "Focus on the Family" program is carried on 1,425 stations, thirty minutes daily, six and sometimes seven days per week. The ministry publishes five magazines, reaching some two million homes per month, and on it goes. Nearly $56 million per year is needed to meet the needs of families. Still, Dobson has never taken a dime in salary since the beginning of the ministry, and he has no intention of ever doing so. Surely, God has blessed that courageous move from the relative safety of Children's Hospital to the uncharted waters of a family ministry.

Anyone wanting to understand what is occurring today in Pomona, California, or more importantly, *why* it is happening, must know what I'm about to share, for Dobson feels it is the heart and soul of the ministry. From the videotaping of the first film series in 1978 until 1985, Dobson restricted his travel severely and depended on the media to convey his ideas. Radio, television, films, books, videotapes, and audio cassettes took the place of airports, pulpits, and seminars. But as the years unfolded, his friends and advisors began suggesting that Dobson prepare a new film series to follow the *Focus on the Family* phenomenon. This original product was now looking very dated. Jim's long sideburns and four-inch-wide ties were grating on his nerves. "If you watch the films very closely," he complained, "you can see the sideburns actually growing on the screen!"

Finally, Dobson began speaking again in preparation for the filming of a new series entitled *Turn Your Heart Toward Home.* In fact, the experience at McNichols Arena in Denver, mentioned in the first chapter, was one of the events scheduled for this purpose. Regardless of their size, the auditoriums were almost always full when the big night arrived. Approximately 15,000 heard Jim and Shirley in Seattle; 8,000 in Fort Wayne; 13,000 in Phoenix; 19,000 in Denver; and 11,000 in Boise. It was an exciting era, but Dobson was climbing back on the old treadmill again.

Overcommitment is an insidious problem for those who are vulnerable to it. They can effectively say no for months or even years and keep their lives under control but then create complete chaos in a single afternoon. This is especially true when one is responding to next year's requests. "Sure, I can do that!" they say, not realizing that "next year" will come down upon them quickly, like a rainstorm.

This is what happened to Jim Dobson in 1985. Focus on the Family was still burgeoning. Just staying on top of its needs was like riding a Brahma bull. By this time, however, he was also deeply committed to serving on various governmental boards and commissions. President Reagan appointed him to the National Advisory Commission on Juvenile Justice and Delinquency Prevention and then began asking him to come to the White House to consult on family-related matters. All these activities, while worthy in themselves, laid a foundation of fatigue, which became difficult to shake.

Also that year Dobson was appointed to the Attorney General's Commission on Pornography, which became an extremely difficult and depressing responsibility. For fifteen months he was exposed to the most wretched and violent material ever produced by mankind. He was also attacked and ridiculed by the forces of darkness which profited from obscenity. The psychological and physical consequences of these experiences weighed heavily on his mind.

As exhaustion accumulated in this man, he began to question the ministry of Focus on the Family. Contributions had unexpectedly plummeted for the first time in its history, running a $750,000 shortfall in two months. Perhaps listeners had heard enough of James Dobson and his guests. When the organization was created back in 1977, Dobson had told the Board he would never beg or plead for money. He believed if he were diligent about meeting human needs, God's people would provide the necessary finances. If they did not, it must mean the Lord had other things for him to do. Maybe it was time to move on.

Could Dobson really have walked away from a ministry that he had founded and nurtured? Yes, if he felt God was no longer in it. The false impression exists, especially since the collapse of the PTL enterprise, that Christian radio and television ministries spring inevitably from the unbridled egomania of their founders. Whether or not that perception is valid in other contexts, Dobson established Focus on the Family on a different footing. The organization does not bear his name and is not a monument to his memory. Instead, he says, "This ministry was organized to serve the family and those in need. When it ceases to function as designed, it should quickly pass from the scene." Remember, also, that this man walked out of Children's Hospital at the peak of his success there.

As Dobson contemplated his circumstances in 1985, a letter arrived unexpectedly from his uncle's sister, Mrs. Aleen Swann. She explained that she had wanted to convey a message to Jim for the past eight years but was impressed to remain silent. Finally she felt the time was right to reveal an event that had occurred in 1977. Her brother (Jim's uncle), Dr. James McGraw, was dying of cancer at the time. She recalled how Dr. Dobson's father had come to the hospital to be near his brother-in-law during his final hours. As they sat in the family room outside the intensive care unit, the elder Dobson shared something that she had kept to herself during the intervening years.

James Dobson, Sr. told her he had been determined that his brother-in-law would not die! As ministers, the two of them had devoted their lives to the propagation of the gospel, and there was much more work to be done. Thus, Rev. Dobson had begun a long vigil before the Lord, asking Him not only to spare Dr. McGraw's life, but to let them both continue in His service for a few more years.

For two days and nights, Rev. Dobson prayed earnestly about this matter. Then as the sun was rising on the morning of the third day, God spoke to him. It was not an audible voice, but the message was unmistakable. He said, "I have heard your prayers. I know that you love Me and are concerned about My people and My kingdom. I have seen your compassion, and I am going to answer your petitions in a way you could never have imagined. You are going to reach literally millions of people for me, from coast to coast and around the world. But it will not be through your efforts or the work of James McGraw. It will be through your *son!*"

That afternoon Dr. James McGraw quietly slipped across the chilly waters of death and into the presence of his Maker. He had been in a deep coma for days, but as he died, he smiled as though greeting a cherished friend. The next day Rev. James Dobson suffered a massive heart attack from which he never recovered. As he was dying, he also smiled after being without a heartbeat for several minutes. He and his beloved brother-in-law had gone to a better world, leaving their labor to the next generation.

As Jim Dobson sat and read the letter from Aleen Swann in 1985, his questions about the ministry of Focus on the Family were answered. Suddenly, he saw the entire effort in a new light. He understood for the first time that its success and influence were not products of his own creativity. They were manifestations of God's blessing and promises to his father. Only from that perspective could he explain the way doors had always opened at precisely the right moment and why such wise decisions had been made when, in retrospect, the real issues were not even comprehended. Clearly, the Lord seemed to be at the helm of the ministry.

"I came to realize," Dobson says, "that my task as the leader of Focus on the Family was simply to avoid doing anything stupid. That may be my primary contribution when it's all said and done."

The last line of Aleen Swann's letter read, "The end is not yet!" She was certainly right. Contributions to the ministry increased dramatically the month after she wrote, and the ministry is now double the size it was in 1985. Fortunately James Dobson has learned to delegate. The Lord has brought to Focus on the Family some very gifted and creative leaders. And the influence of Rev. Dobson's only son continues to escalate. It does appear, indeed, that *the end is not yet!*

7

Setting the Standard

In his role as head of a new ministry, Dr. Dobson began to implement the key principles and administrative concepts that would guide his efforts for years to come. He came to the task with a catalog of convictions about ethics and integrity that he has followed from the very first day. Chief among them is his perspective on money.

He is firmly convinced that the way an organization handles its finances is a reflection of its integrity in *every* area. Therefore, he established strict limitations on the way Focus on the Family would solicit contributions and on the way money would be used. These are the policies that have guided the ministry from the early days, as written by James Dobson.

1. This ministry belongs to God, not to James Dobson. It is neither a monument to my ego nor a legacy to my memory. Focus on the Family does not bear my name . . . the buildings are not dedicated to me . . . we have not founded a James Dobson University. I am merely a fellow-servant in the work of the kingdom.

2. The Lord has apparently chosen to place His mantle of approval on the ministry of Focus on the Family. Nevertheless, He gives and sometimes takes away. If He ever closes the doors to this work, we will accept His leadings

and yield the outcome to Him. Until then, we will devote every ounce of energy to the task at hand.

3. One of the ways we can discern the Lord's will regarding the continuation of our work is through the support He sends (or doesn't send) from His people. Therefore, during lean times we will make our obligations known to our friends—but we will not squirm, scratch or claw for contributions. We will never resort to what we consider to be disrespectful and dishonorable methods of fundraising, even when the needs are serious.

4. We will ask people not to support Focus on the Family or any other Christian program until their obligations to the local church have been met. The church is the first line of defense for the family.

5. We will not *operate* the ministry at a deficit. Although from time to time it is necessary to borrow funds for large capital expenditures, such as for a new building, we will seek to repay the loan as soon as possible.

6. We consider the contributions we receive to be "blood money"—sent from loving people who have sacrificed to make their gifts possible. Our obligation, therefore, is to spend that money conservatively and wisely in continuing the ministry. We have no limousines or airplanes or condos in Hawaii. Every penny is stretched as far as possible to serve the needs of today's families.

7. We will receipt all donations showing the value of any materials sent in order to help contributors determine the tax-deductible portion of their gifts. (The Internal Revenue Code permits donors to deduct the amount they give to Focus on the Family in excess of the value of materials received from the organization.)

8. When we make a purchase, we will pay the invoice within thirty days if possible. We do not intend to use the vendor's money.

9. We will not try to raise more money than we need.

10. I will not be the primary fund-raiser.

11. Shirley and I will accept no salary for this work and will pay a portion of the radio airtime expenses to compensate for the publicity that increases our book sales. When our books are offered to our listeners, we will waive all royalty to allow Focus to obtain the lowest possible price from the publisher.

12. We will never sell or rent our mailing list to those wishing to use the names and addresses of our supporters. Those individuals contacted us in good faith, and if they wanted to receive mail from other organizations, I'm sure they would ask for it. We will maintain the tightest security on our list of friends and supporters.

13. We will conform to the standards established by the Evangelical Council for Financial Accountability—the Christian organization created to assure ethical monetary practices.

   To summarize, we will try to remember always that Jesus Christ is our possessor and our dispossessor. He ordained and blessed this ministry. It belongs entirely to Him.

Public response to these policy statements has been most gratifying, especially item eight. As you may know, it is customary for companies to delay paying invoices as long as possible in order to earn interest or otherwise use other companies' money. When it is recognized that Focus will not engage in such practices, it is not unusual to receive an expression of surprise and appreciation—often from secular vendors. It is one way of testifying to our Christian faith. Such a letter was sent to us by a vendor recently, for example, and it is reproduced below with the permission of the writer.

I'm writing today to *thank you* for the many years I have served Focus on the Family's printing needs. More importantly, I want to thank you for impacting the lives of our employees and me. Focus on the Family has demonstrated the difference between operating in the love of God and operating under the authority of the almighty dollar.

Shortly after calling on Focus on the Family in 1983, I gave my life to the Lord. I saw something different at Focus on the Family that I didn't see at my other accounts. I observed love in action, tremendous concern for fellow human beings, and higher ethics than the "world" required. I wanted so much to be a part of this "different" lifestyle.

As Exec-U-Forms was started, our accounting staff also saw a difference in Focus on the Family. You always paid on time. Six and one-half years later, Exec-U-Forms now services over 200 customers, and the same is still true. Focus on the Family is one account we can *always* rely on for on-time payments. Your organization has demonstrated uncompromising Christian ethics.

Recently, we had some setbacks when my father, Chuck Thomas, had to go to the hospital for an emergency operation. Your staff only knew of his illness through conversations with myself. Yet, they mailed to him, a man they did not even know, get-well cards signed personally with a little note from each staff member. My father does not know the Lord, but the night before his operation for the first time since I have been saved, he let me pray for him.

Thank you again for sharing Jesus Christ with our company.

God bless you all,

Ron Whalen
President

Paul Nelson, who currently serves as executive vice-president of Focus on the Family, observed Dobson's careful attitudes toward money during his early days on the staff. Focus had just gone through its most severe financial nose dive in history, leading Jim to write a monthly letter that spelled out the need. He did not beg for money, but he made it clear that contributions were running nearly $400,000 per month below expenses. In response, giving increased dramatically during the next sixty days. Dobson then wrote his constituency again, telling them that the crisis had passed and thanking them for their generosity.

Nelson recalls a meeting where Dobson, he, and I were discussing this letter. Nelson remembers me telling Dobson, "You realize that contributions to the ministry may fall off a cliff again if you tell people there is no more need." The summer months were still ahead, and I was afraid the financial slump would recur.

107

Dobson replied, "I am aware of that, Rolf, but there are three reasons why I think we should tell everyone that the need has been met. First, I think many well-intentioned people may have diverted their tithe money to help us in a pinch, even though I have repeatedly told them not to do so. I don't want to redirect any more money from local churches. Second, I know that there are other ministries which are hurting financially. Every time we ask our donors to give a little extra, I'm aware that we're probably diverting money away from these organizations that are equally deserving. Third, our needs have been met for now. It is proper that we should thank our donors and not ask for more money than we really need."

This reaction had a profound impact on Nelson, who told me, "At that moment I became convinced of Dobson's integrity."

Dr. Dobson's strong convictions about ethics do not end with the proper handling of finances, of course. They extend to every dimension of the ministry. To best understand that philosophy, perhaps it would be helpful to read about it in his own words:

The year was 1976, and I was in Atlantic City, New Jersey, for the Christian Booksellers Association convention. I had been asked to speak during the banquet on the final evening and had arrived a few days early to get the "feel" of the event. I'll never forget what happened that afternoon as I walked among the rows of booths provided by Christian publishers. My books and tapes were scattered here and there, and a large photograph of me was positioned near the center of one display. As I crossed an aisle near the north end of the convention hall, the Lord spoke to me.

Rarely do I ever say, "God told me" or "God said. . . ." It is a dangerous thing to put words in the mouth of the Almighty, and I am extremely cautious in making such a statement. But there are times when you *know* you have heard from Him, even though there are no audible words. That is what happened in Atlantic City. And this is what the Lord said to me on that afternoon (as expressed in human terms):

Jim, you can see that I have chosen to make you visible and influential among my people for purposes that you may not comprehend. In so doing, I am making My Kingdom *vulnerable* to you. You will be able to hurt and disappoint the family of believers by the things you do and say. *Don't mess it up!* Bridle your tongue.

108

Guard your behavior. Raise your ethical standard. Protect my people!

Though I didn't fully understand in 1976 why the Lord was dealing with me so emphatically, the meaning has become clear in the intervening years. Focus on the Family was launched just seven months later, thrusting Shirley and me into the public arena. Then in 1979, the first film series was to make our little family recognizable throughout Christendom. It seems obvious today that the Lord was preparing me for the dramatic changes that were about to revolutionize my life.

Now, more than thirteen years later, the warning I received in Atlantic City still rings in my ears. My greatest fear is that my inadequacies and imperfections will lead me to do something to hurt the cause of Christ. It could happen so easily, despite my determination to avoid a major blunder. When one becomes very visible in the Christian community, especially in today's environment, every step can be on a land mine. I'm not talking about the kind of evil that devastated other large ministries in recent years. Though it could happen to us, I have no intention of committing deliberate and blatant misconduct. But there are other insidious dangers lurking in the shadows, such as a major financial mistake, or an on-air blunder, or the press distortions of a Bundy-like episode (referring to mass murderer Theodore Bundy) or even a lawsuit in this litigious society. I am keenly aware that Satan *hates* this ministry and he will do anything he can, not only to bring it down, but to discredit the Kingdom in the process. I tell you from my heart that I had rather never been born than to bring reproach on the community of believers and the faith of our fathers.

King David did just that by his adultery with Bathsheba and the murder of her faithful husband, Uriah. The king was successful in hiding his sin from everyone but the Lord, Who sent Nathan the prophet to say, "Thou Art the Man!" Then Nathan said something to David that has reverberated down through the corridors of time: ". . . by this deed you have given great occasion to the enemies of the Lord to blaspheme . . ." (2 Sam. 12:14 NKJV).

Isn't that what has happened through the years when well-known and influential ministers commit highly publicized sin? When it occurs today, comedians like Johnny Carson and David Letterman are given a great occasion to blaspheme the name of our Savior. It *must* not happen again!

As I see it, the greatest threat to the ministry of Focus on the Family is that we who lead it might begin to believe our own press. Egos being what they are, the natural inclination is to take personal credit for any successes coming our way. But we know the dangers of that error. Every positive thing that has happened in our thirteen-year history has been a direct consequence of God's blessing. If He ever removes His hand of mercy from us, we will flounder helplessly in a sea of futility.

Another Old Testament character makes this point all too clearly. King Nebuchadnezzar was extremely impressed by his earthly accomplishments, and humanly speaking, he had every right to be proud. He had conquered the entire civilized world and made slaves and servants out of all his enemies. No one could oppose or defy him with an impunity. Then one fateful night, he contemplated his own magnificence while he strolled on the roof of his palace. As he surveyed the city below him, he said to himself: "Is not this great Babylon, that I have built for a royal dwelling by my mighty power and for the honor of my majesty?" (Dan. 4:30 NKJV).

That's all it took. While the words were still in Nebuchadnezzar's mouth, he literally became psychotic. He wandered into the fields where he ate grass like the oxen. We then read in verse 33, "his body was wet with the dew of heaven till his hair had grown like eagles' *feathers* and his nails like birds' *claws*" [italics added].

God *will not* tolerate haughty pride and self-sufficiency. We see the validity of that statement throughout Scripture. Remember the example of King Herod, who became one of the most wicked despots of all times. He killed the Apostle James, arrested Peter, and persecuted the early church viciously. Nevertheless, he escaped the wrath of God for a time.

Then one day he crossed the line. He permitted his subjects to proclaim him a god and not a man. Suddenly, death came knocking at his door. The Scripture says, "then immediately an angel of the Lord struck him, because he did not give glory to God. And he was eaten by worms and died" (Acts 12:23 NKJV).

It is a fearful thing to claim for oneself the majesty and honor that belongs to the Most Holy God! But why do I write these thoughts in reference to Focus on the Family? Because I firmly believe that those of us who are called to positions of Christian leadership are held to a higher standard of holiness (James 3:1). In short, our accountability is not only to our Board of Directors and to those who support the ministry, but also to the King of kings and Lord of lords. What an awesome thought!

That's why I'm asking you to pray consistently and specifically for this ministry. Plead with the Lord on our behalf, first that He will keep this work untarnished and clean, and second, that He will give strength and wisdom to those of us in positions of leadership. The burden continues to be very heavy on all of us.

Another early commitment by James Dobson was that Focus on the Family was to be first and foremost a Christian ministry. That is, he decided the effort to reach out to families through Christian media would never be overridden by secular opportunities that came along. And come along they did.

In early 1983, Dr. Dobson was invited to be a guest on the Larry King Show, which he accepted. On the basis of his response there, the president of the Mutual Broadcasting Network, the largest system of commercial stations in the country, asked Dobson and his leadership team to come to their corporate offices in Washington, D.C. They wanted to discuss the possibility of a new radio series to be produced by Focus on the Family and aired throughout the Mutual network.

Intrigued by the possibility of creating a special program that potentially would reach millions of unchurched people, Dr. Dobson accepted the invitation. The meeting took place in the executive conference room of Mutual's plush corporate headquarters. After exchanging some complimentary remarks, the president laid his proposal on the table. He suggested that Dr. Dobson cancel his current program on Christian radio in order to devote himself to a new, daily, secular series, including broadcasts on Sunday. The implication was that by doing so he could become a major personality on American radio.

Dr. Dobson listened to the promising proposition and then politely declined the offer on the spot. He later explained his reasoning: "I believe that God has called me first to strengthen the Christian home. We may have the opportunity some day to reach a broader audience, but it will never be at the expense of that primary ministry to Christians."

There were two other reasons he had declined the offer, which could have made him a wealthy man. First, he would have been required to broadcast four hours on Sunday, which is a family time and a church day for him. And second, commercial sponsorship would have prohibited Dr. Dobson from talking specifically about his faith. That was out of the question.

During my association with Jim Dobson, I have witnessed

other situations where the secular media have enticed him with the prospects of speaking to a national audience. That is simply not a major objective for him. He routinely turns down guest appearances on "Nightline" with Ted Koppel, "Crossfire," and other programs. After the interview with condemned killer Ted Bundy in 1989, more than nine hundred requests for interviews came his way in a span of four days. "CBS Morning News" offered to send a private jet to pick him up and then deliver him wherever he wanted to go. The same morning, "The Today Show," "Good Morning America," and virtually every syndicated talk program in the country was in the queue. Dobson tested the waters by accepting four local television interviews in Florida. Once he saw how the press was going to use him to distort Bundy's statement, he promptly declined the rest.

The producers of these shows can't understand Dr. Dobson's independence, of course. Most people dream about the kind of instant notoriety they offer. Some actively seek it. But until he feels the Lord directing him otherwise, Dobson is content to convey his thoughts to the Christian community.

That opportunity has been possible through the marvelous industry of religious radio stations. While that may be taken for granted in the United States, it is a liberty not enjoyed in most countries—including many in the Western world such as Canada, Great Britain, and Australia. In those nations, the government controls the radio airwaves and severely limits Christian programming. But in America, we have more than two thousand stations that are operated for the sole purpose of disseminating the gospel, which is due in large part to the First Amendment and to the fact that many of the first radio stations in this country were pioneered by evangelists and preachers.

When Dobson decided to use that medium, he committed himself to creating the most helpful and interesting radio programs possible. And the Lord blessed these efforts as the ministry continued to grow. Hundreds of religious stations began carrying the "Focus on the Family" broadcast. Soon it was heard in every metropolitan center in the country.

Al Sanders, president of Ambassador Advertising and the unofficial "dean" of Christian radio, was astounded at the unexpected expansion. He had never seen a program proliferate so quickly. Certainly, one reason for the widespread success was Dobson's uniqueness. There was nothing like his program in religious radio, which was basically characterized at the time by preachers who packaged their Sunday sermons for the airwaves. True, many radio and television ministers were teaching general scriptural principles related to family life, but few were addressing the broad range of specific problems confronting real people in everyday situations.

Al Sanders explained the phenomenon: "In those days, Christian radio programming was back-to-back pulpit thumpers. Jim Dobson brought a relief from that intensity of preaching. He also gave the practical application that so many sermons were missing."

Sanders' belief in the validity of this ministry was more than just lip service. Throughout the early years, his agency provided its assistance to Dobson at a financial loss so that Focus on the Family could afford it.

As a result of Dr. Dobson's success, Sanders feels the entire religious broadcast industry has been affected positively. "Today, the whole genre of Christian talk radio is a result of Dr. Dobson's impact," Sanders says. "The call-in programs, the feature magazine formats, and the interview shows are byproducts of the influence of 'Focus on the Family.'"

Aside from God's obvious blessing, one of the most significant principles that has helped Jim Dobson is his tireless commitment to high standards in broadcast preparations. He still devotes an average of two hours of his time and ten hours of his programming staff's time for every thirty minutes on the air.

When Al Sanders initially learned of this, he tried to convince Jim this was unnecessary. "You're taking too much time to put these shows together!" Sanders exclaimed. "Just go into the studio, turn on the microphone, and start talking. You can get it done in one-fourth the time."

Sanders is now glad that Dobson ignored his advice. "Jim's commitment to perfection, broadcast integrity, and production quality set him apart," Sanders said. "In fact, he caused other Christian broadcasters to question their own standards, and that has lifted the entire industry." Dobson has not accomplished this alone. He has been assisted in the studio by co-host Mike Trout, a gifted broadcast professional. Behind them are a number of other talented individuals who ply their skills in programming and production. All of them help the psychologist produce the best possible programs.

Of course, the more Dobson worked at it, the better he became. As the result of his proficiency and success as a broadcaster, many have sought to imitate him. "I get calls almost every day from psychologists and counselors who tell me that they want to start a program like Dobson's," Sanders says. "They talk as though it were some kind of formula. But in addition to his credentials, high standards, and hard work, Jim has something else going that few people can duplicate. He has the ability to convey his sincerity through the radio microphone. He is the most believable person on the air."

This points to another principle behind Dobson's success as a communicator. He is extremely sensitive to the needs of his listeners. After launching his program, he seldom had time to speak publicly and to meet people face to face. This used to give him an opportunity to hear their concerns. But he now had another means to stay in touch with his audience. The daily mail became his stethoscope to hear the heartbeat of his constituents.

From the earliest days of his broadcast ministry, he selected program topics on the basis of the letters he received. His listeners' needs were reflected by some of the early program titles:

Coping with Toddlerhood

Living with an Unsaved Spouse

The Lure of Infidelity

Teen Rebellion

To Spank or Not to Spank

Preparing for College

Traditional Values in Education

Sports and Your Child

Even the decision to create a daily half-hour broadcast was predicated on the interests of his listeners. He began the radio ministry as a weekly effort, but that allowed him to cover only forty-five topics each year. By contrast, letters he received from his listeners suggested hundreds of subjects relating to marriage, parenthood, child development, emotions, learning disabilities, social issues, government intervention, abortion, aging, sexual problems, Christian education, drug abuse, adolescence, meno-pause, mid-life crisis, and singleness. Before long he realized it would require decades to deal with the hundreds of subjects requested by his listeners. So he expanded the broadcast from a weekly program to a daily program of fifteen minutes, and then to a thirty-minute format in late 1981.

But neither a daily broadcast nor the monthly magazine he launched could adequately meet the needs expressed in the sacks of mail that arrived each day on his doorstep. Letter after letter told stories of marital conflict, suffering children, incest, disease, and heartache. On any given day you could dip your hand into that sack of mail and read the most heart-wrenching personal accounts imaginable, such as these actual examples:

• A woman confessed for the first time that she was the tragic victim of her father's perverted sexual experiments. He was ad-dicted to hard-core pornography, and throughout her childhood he subjected her to perform the acts he saw depicted on the pages of these obscene magazines. She had never told anyone of these experiences and had been suffering severe emotional trauma throughout her adult life.

• A family related how they had just taken into their home four little children who had been abandoned by their stepfather when their mother died of cancer. Prior to her death, she had married four men in succession. When she died, her latest hus-band simply stepped out of the responsibility of being a father and left his stepchildren destitute.

• Another woman chronicled an entire lifetime of pain on a seventy-five-foot roll of freezer paper. She started her handwrit-ten scroll with these words: "No one cares." She had experienced enough hurt and rejection in her life to fill the entire roll.

Because Dr. Dobson could not address these needs through the "visible" avenue of his ministry (broadcasting and publications), he developed another level of outreach that might well be called the "invisible" ministry. This part of the organization often comes as a surprise to the casual observer. In fact, visitors to Focus on the Family's headquarters have always been surprised to see the entire program in operation. Today, it involves a highly dedicated staff working on behalf of families in 250,000 square feet of office space in Pomona, California.

Many of these people work in the "invisible" or "hidden" departments that quietly labor to provide needed assistance to those who write. For example, a valiant effort is being made to answer the thousands of questions asked every day. A pastor in Seattle may write us to say, "Our local school district is considering adoption of a policy that will allow homosexual counselors on campus. Where can we obtain information to refute the propaganda that the gay community is presenting to the school board?"

Or a mother may ask, "Where can I get psychological testing for my daughter? After hearing your program today, I think she may be suffering from dyslexia."

Dobson created a staff to research the answers to questions like these and to respond quickly. *Every* letter receives the best answer the organization is capable of sending. There are no quick form letters to brush off the writer. Each one is taken seriously; in fact, it is common to see a staff member bow in prayer before responding to a difficult letter.

Because many of the letters, like the examples above, include questions about serious counseling matters, Dr. Dobson has personally written or edited more than nine hundred letters that serve as models when professional advice is needed. He also retains a staff of licensed marriage, family, and child counselors to deal with the most desperate problems. Theirs has been an impossible task, of course, since no ministry can undertake to counsel the entire nation—especially by mail or phone.

But since the earliest days of the organization, Dr. Dobson has insisted that those hidden efforts also operate according to the highest standards in order to help as many people as possible. Through every dimension of the ministry, he demands quality— not for its own sake, but so people will be treated properly. Nothing upsets him more than to learn that a desperate letter has been ignored or a phone call has not been returned. Treating someone with discourtesy is one of the few mistakes that will raise his blood pressure.

"The problem," he says, "is that people draw conclusions about the validity of our testimony from the way we respond to their needs. If the person who answers the phone is rude, or if the accounting department fails to pay an invoice on time, or if we mishandle a letter, those who have been rebuffed will conclude, 'Dobson sounded okay on the radio, like he really cares, but he is just another phony who is in it for himself.'

"In other words, our failures become a slur—not on our own names—but on the gospel itself. We represent Jesus Christ in every transaction, in every corner of this ministry. Therefore, our standard must be nothing short of excellence."

This principle of meeting human needs has been the hallmark of Focus on the Family through the years. Never in its existence have its executives sat around a conference table saying, "How can we grow? How can we build this ministry?" Instead, the question has been, "A new need is being brought to our door. What are we going to do about it?" That philosophy of *service* to all comers explains the unprecedented growth of the ministry. When an organization hangs out a shingle saying, "We care for you," it will prosper. That is true of a business, a resort, and particularly a church. There are simply too few givers to go around, and the world will beat a path to their door.

This philosophy, which has been evident in Focus on the Family since its inception, is highly dependent on *feedback* from those being served. A marksman can't improve his aim if he never knows where the shots are hitting. Consequently, Dobson places the highest priority on listening to those who contact him.

To fulfill this objective, he devised a "Crits" report that excerpts comments from letters that are critical of him or the ministry. He takes that report very seriously, reading it cover to cover every month. He is determined to meet needs and wants to know how he can serve his constituents better. He also receives a report of telephone calls coming into the ministry each week, which he goes over with a fine-toothed comb. This assures him that the ministry is meeting needs, that people are being treated right, and that the constituency's ideas for improvement get a fair hearing.

This sensitivity to criticism and to suggestions stands in stark contrast to the practice of a popular television ministry whose vice-president visited our offices one day. During the course of our conversation with this gentleman, Dr. Dobson asked him, "What does your president do with the letters from people who say they tried to follow his particular teachings but found they didn't work?"

"He doesn't do anything with them because we don't show them to him," the vice-president said. "If he saw complaints, he would become discouraged and lose his confidence. We can't afford for that to happen."

In other words, an entire ministry (which shall remain nameless) has been built around the particular teachings of one man whose subordinates shelter him from the truthful feedback of his supporters. Can you imagine any business succeeding without ever benefiting from customer complaints? I can't recall a single major hotel chain I have visited that didn't provide a customer survey in its rooms. Frequent fliers are accustomed to filling out forms to evaluate the airline. New car buyers receive similar polls within weeks after making their purchase. "How were you treated by the salesman? What was the condition of your car upon delivery? How is it operating? How has the service department treated you?"

Dobson applies the same strategy to running the ministry. He is determined to know as much as he can about his organization and the people it serves. When the volume of mail exceeded his ability to read each letter, he established more systems and reports to ensure that he had an accurate reading of his constituency's pulse and how they were being treated.

He even began testing the system by asking friends to write to Focus on the Family. He wanted to know how quickly they received a response and whether or not it adequately answered their questions. He has also been known to stop by the office on Saturdays and open mail himself just to ensure he was not losing touch with the expanding audience reaching out to him.

He applied this standard to others as well. Recently, we were

118

approached by another ministry seeking help from Focus on the Family. They were unaware that part of our consideration of their request depended on the outcome of a test we conducted on their mail-response systems. Before Dobson would commit to an ongoing relationship with this ministry, he wanted to know how they treated people. This one criterion tells a great deal about an organization's attitudes toward serving others.

Dobson implemented other procedures in order to run Focus on the Family with businesslike efficiency. He surrounded himself with people whom he judged to be "detail oriented." At our headquarters, leadership positions are reserved for those who take notes, follow through on assignments, and return their phone calls. New employees have often remarked that the Focus "culture" is characterized by high energy meetings where staff members record their assignments on yellow legal pads. If Dobson gives an assignment to an uninitiated staff member who simply nods in understanding, Dobson will ask the person to *write down* the instruction. "No one has *that* good a memory," he says.

In 1986, Dobson articulated his philosophy about details in the following memo that was sent to all staff members.

Let me express a philosophy about which I feel *very* strongly. Focus on the Family is a *detail* organization. The amount of mail we receive and the lives we touch have made us a ministry to more than 900,000 people . . . almost a million families that ask for our assistance and share their burdens with us day after day. Furthermore, the various activities and programs we offer are composed of countless individual parts that must all be accounted for if we are to do the job efficiently. Therefore, I must emphasize that there is *NO* place in this ministry for any employee who is unwilling to chase detail. From vice-presidents to the newest hourly employee, we all must be willing to pay that price. I have profound respect for the people who pay our bills, and we *will not* treat them shabbily. For every letter which sits on someone's desk, there is a person somewhere who feels insulted or rejected or angry at us for our lack of consideration.

Come on, folks. Let's put this problem behind us. Detail! Detail! Detail! Detail! Detail! I know it's frustrating, and I'm drowning in it. But if I can chase it, you can, too. If not, you're working in the wrong organization.

Not only is Dr. Dobson himself highly organized, but he has a reputation at Focus for being a problem-solver who seeks quick resolutions to dilemmas. If you invite him to a meeting, be prepared for him to jump to the board in the middle of the discussion. Armed with a piece of chalk or a Magic Marker, he will quickly write down all possible options or form a "pros" and "cons" list. In this manner, he often leads his staff toward the best solution.

Another Dobson concept has become legendary at Focus on the Family. It's called "mutual accountability." Though it sounds like a financial bookkeeping system, it actually governs the way staff members relate to one another. Each vice-president is responsible for running his own particular department, but not exclusively. He is accountable in that assignment not only to Dobson and to Paul Nelson, the executive vice-president, but also to all the other vice-presidents. There are no exclusive territories at Focus that are "owned" by a single individual. Why is this necessary? Dobson has observed that ministries and businesses often get into trouble because the chief executive officer becomes too busy to know what is going on. One or more of his subordinates begins to make drastic mistakes or to commit the organization to activities that threaten its very existence.

How many times have you heard a leader say, "I had no idea my v.p. of finance (or whoever) had spent $250,000 without our authorization. We were bankrupt before we knew it"?

Dobson's protection against that danger is to permit *no* unilateral decisions of consequence in the ministry. No one, not even Dobson himself, makes major decisions in private. Everything of significance is brought to a weekly cabinet meeting, where all the ramifications are carefully examined and discussed. The result is lengthy meetings that could be avoided, but the payoff is in the quality of the organization. By God's grace Focus on the Family has made very few really awful mistakes. Mutual accountability has also diminished some of the territorial walls between departments that spring up when independent and secretive endeavors are permitted. Mutual accountability is an inefficient, but *very* secure, system!

Remarkably, James Dobson is also determined to keep

up with his own staff members—all 640 of them. While he is unable to have an "open door policy" with every employee, he visits departments when he can, and he listens to the employees. If he hears about a morale problem in a given area, he will ask the supervisor to be absent while he listens to the staff. In the monthly chapel services when all employees are assembled, Dobson will sometimes have microphones set up in the aisles and permit anyone to ask him any question he or she wishes. Finally, he reads *every* report written by every employee who leaves the organization. Each employee who resigns is asked to evaluate the ministry as a place of work, to rate his supervisor, and to cite any grievances or complaints. If trouble exists in an area, James Dobson will soon know about it.

Another important principle that has guided the ministry is actually an extension of Dobson's personal generosity. Every person who is well acquainted with Jim Dobson is aware of this characteristic. Peb Jackson recalls this incident:

"I was in Washington, D.C. a few years ago and had the assignment to meet Jim at National Airport. I jumped into a cab at my hotel and noticed that the African taxi driver was listening to a religious station. So I asked him if he ever listened to the 'Focus on the Family' broadcast. 'Oh, yes,' responded the man in broken English. 'I listen to Dr. Dobson every day.'

"When I told him we were on our way to meet Dr. Dobson, he became so excited he could hardly keep his car on the road! On our way back to the hotel, Jim struck up a conversation with the driver and learned that he had come from Nairobi to study in America. When Jim discovered that this student was having financial problems and was trying to save enough money to see his family in Nairobi, Jim pulled out his checkbook and wrote the young man a personal check for $300. It's typical of him to do that," Peb says.

I remember an instance when one of our employees approached Dr. Dobson with a question about our benevolence policy. The local police had informed us that a man in the area was visiting churches and ministries looking for handouts. The police advised us to ignore him. "Should we curtail our assistance program?" the employee asked. Jim's answer was as predictable as the rising sun. He said, "God doesn't require us to qualify the recipients of our generosity. He will bless us for meeting this need."

If you understand the principles by which James Dobson lives, you can predict his behavior. He holds certain convictions so deeply you know he will never violate them. Some members of the staff who seem frequently to spark his irritation see him as difficult to please. In truth, they have never really understood the principles by which he operates: attention to detail, respect for every person who reaches out to us, avoiding waste, and the desire for superior quality in everything bearing the Focus name. If you know these cherished ideals and implement them, James Dobson is an easy man to work for.

Another significant spiritual practice that has worked its way into the daily regimen of Focus on the Family is Jim's deep commitment to prayer. Each workday morning the entire Focus staff pauses for twenty minutes of devotions. It's undoubtedly a source of frustration for people who try to call a staff member during this period, but it has become an inviolable practice. Every Wednesday that devotional time is set aside to pray specifically for the prayer requests in letters received by the ministry. The staff prays for each need and each person, by name, in those letters. This also stands in contrast to some ministries that reportedly dump letters with prayer requests on the floor and ask God to meet the needs represented in the pile.

One of the most memorable demonstrations of the Lord's blessing in response to Dobson's prayer commitment occurred in early 1981. The staff was working shoulder to shoulder in a cramped building on First Street in Arcadia. The crowded conditions had begun to affect adversely the group's productivity.

Mac McQuiston was assigned to search for a larger facility we could lease. At the same time, Dr. Dobson became aware of some property available at 41 E. Foothill Boulevard in Arcadia. Because the ministry operated on a subsistence basis and most of the funds were being funneled into the purchase of airtime, they never dreamed they could own their own building.

But Mac told Jim simply, "Let's go up and ask God to give it to us." They quickly called Board member Dr. Mike Roberts, a local dentist at the time, and he joined them within minutes at the site.

Another meeting with the President in the Oval Office.

Dr. Dobson (to the President's left) at a White House meeting in 1984. They were discussing this question: "What can government do to assist the family?"

Jim and Shirley with the President.

Attorney General Edwin Meese's Commission on Pornography in 1985. This eleven-member body worked for 15 months without pay, and then was promptly sued by *Playboy* and *Penthouse* magazines. The issue was still not resolved three years later.

Dr. Dobson meeting privately with then Vice President George Bush, in 1988.

Former Secretary of the Interior, Don Hodel, enjoyed a hot morning of basketball with Jim in a Washington, D.C. gymnasium.

Dobson has been an outdoorsman since childhood, and fly fishing remains a favorite form of recreation.

Dobson with friend Chuck Swindoll on a Canadian fishing trip.

Jim and Senior Vice President, Peb Jackson, on a quail hunting trip.

The Dobsons in 1985.

The Dobsons celebrate their 25th anniversary with Shirley's parents, Joe and Alma Kubishta.

Members of the Focus on the Family staff surprise Jim by visiting his morning basketball game. It was his 50th birthday. Personal Assistant, Dee Otte, is holding the sign and Senior Vice President, Rolf Zettersten, is on her left. Mike Trout, Senior Vice President, is at the far right of the picture.

The Dobsons on a vacation in New England.

Ryan Dobson performs a skateboard stunt in California.

The staff of Focus on the Family in 1987. Two hundred members have joined this team in the past two years.

The central headquarters building of the ministry in Pomona, California.

Dr. Dobson in a counseling session.

Prison Fellowship founder, Chuck Colson, visits the radio studios of Focus on the Family.

Co-host, Mike Trout, and guest Larry Burkett pause for a photograph before going on the air.

Focus on the Family Board Members, Dr. Ted Engstrom and Tony Wauterlek, join Dr. Dobson in breaking ground for a new building.

Mike and Jim on the air.

Jim with the four friends who were soon to die in a terrible plane crash in 1987. From the left, Dr. Trevor Mabery, Hugo Schoellkopf III, Creath Davis and George Clark. It took many months for Dobson to recover from the tragic loss of these beloved friends.

A recent photo of Jim and Shirley near their home in Southern California.

Danae as a college senior, 1988.

Shirley greets children in a Massai tribal village near Nairobi, Kenya.
She and Jim went there in 1988 on a missionary trip.

Ryan after high school graduation.

Danae Dobson on a trip to Australia with her parents in 1989.

Dr. Dobson interviews condemned killer, Ted Bundy, just 17 hours before he was executed in Florida State Prison.

James and Shirley Dobson with Dr. Billy Graham during the Anaheim evangelistic crusade.

Big Jim in Australia, 1989. Note the familiar USC jacket.

Shirley in Australia, 1989.

A beautiful sunset graced that evening as they stood on the newly formed foundation. It must have been a strange sight for the afternoon commuters who saw three men standing in a circle holding hands. But their heads were bowed, and they were oblivious to the cars moving by in the rush-hour traffic. Their thoughts were focused on God as each uttered in his own words this simple prayer: "Lord, give us this property." It was an audacious request and a tremendous step of faith because they had absolutely no money to purchase the building. But six months later, the facility was complete and Focus on the Family occupied half of it. Two years later, as the need grew, Focus owned it all.

One day that same year, Mac suddenly felt a strong burden to fast and pray for three days on behalf of the ministry. He had never done that before, but he followed this leading and told no one about his decision. On the third day of his fast, Mac and Jim met for a prearranged lunch appointment. Mac was about to explain his abstinence from food when Dobson spoke.

"I'd like to eat with you today, Mac, but I'm doing something I've never done before," he said. "I'm fasting for three days and praying for our work."

Mac was shocked. God had directed both of them to devote the same amount of time, during the same week, to intercessory prayer for the well-being of the ministry. During this period of prayer and fasting, Dobson received further confirmation of the Lord's guidance when he came across this verse: ". . . and all the people were very happy because of what God had accomplished so quickly" (2 Chron. 29:36 TLB).

Ever since that day, this has been a theme verse for the ministry. A sign with that Scripture hangs in the lobby and serves as a reminder that the ministry of Focus on the Family belongs to Jesus Christ. Its growth and its success are entirely dependent on Him and adherence to *His* principles.

8

Common Criticisms

Dr. James Dobson and the ministry of Focus on the Family have never been the subject of heated controversy within the Christian community—at least, not to the time of this writing. He receives only two negative letters out of every one thousand arriving at his Pomona headquarters, and some of those are directed at his radio guests. That rather quiet level of criticism is remarkable considering that Dobson addresses many controversial subjects in his broadcasts and writings, including pornography, abortion, and sex education in the schools. Even when people disagree with him, most do not become angry or resentful.

That is certainly *not* true of the media. On at least one occasion, Dr. Dobson created what he called a "feeding frenzy" among members of the working press. In January 1989, mass murderer Ted Bundy asked Dobson to interview him on videotape, just seventeen hours before his execution in the Florida State Prison. They had communicated for more than two years, during which time Bundy made it clear that he wanted to make a statement about pornography and the role it had played in inflaming his deviant sexual passions. Dobson knew the press would try to destroy him if he accepted Bundy's invitation—and he was right. For six weeks after the now famous videotape was recorded, Dobson was made to look like an exploiter, a liar, a fool, and a dishonest "radio evangelist" who interviewed Bundy just for the money. In truth, Focus on the Family executives were offered one-half million dollars for a twenty-four-hour exclusive right to air the tape. Instead they *gave* copies to every member of the press who requested them. Not one cent from the distribution of the video was retained by Dobson.

The Bundy ordeal was a revealing chapter in the history of the American media. Fearing censorship or an invasion of their First Amendment rights, they attempted to drown Bundy's valuable confession in a sea of lies and distortion. Still, the message that they most fear (that there is a link between hardcore, violent pornography and violence against women and children) got past them and was heard by the American public. James Dobson feels it was worth the cost to him to help Bundy tell his terrible story.

However, criticism by the press in the Bundy affair and similar episodes distresses Dobson less than the prospect of controversy within the body of Christ. His greatest concern from the early days has been that he would do something to hurt the cause of Christ and those who are giving their lives to its propagation. He knows that the Christian community has an unfortunate history of elevating common men to the status of heroes and then thrashing them in disgust when they inevitably fail to live up to the standard of perfection. "When you stand on a pedestal," he says, "a step in *any* direction will take you down."

That is why Dobson is uneasy about the influence he has been given. He knows that sooner or later he or a member of his staff will do something—say something—be something—that will anger or disappoint his former admirers. Being on the radio three hours per week, preparing magazines read by millions each month, and now venturing into public policy—all provide opportunities for costly mistakes and failure. Inevitably he will disappoint some people at some point.

But the *personal* ramifications of a fall from prominence don't trouble Dobson. "If the Christian public ever grows weary of my work," he says, "I'll just do something else. To be honest, it would be a bit of a relief to get out from under the pressure."

On the other hand, what *does* alarm Dobson is the potential for satanic mischief among believers. He says, "I am a highly visible Christian leader who could hurt the work of the gospel around the world by my shortcomings. God help me! I am just a man!"

Dobson has been thinking about his vulnerable situation for several years. He came home from a writing trip in 1985 with a Scripture he had seen for the first time. This passage in Ezek. 34:2–10 spoke eloquently of the awesome responsibilities shared by those in positions of leadership:

This is what the Lord God says: How terrible it will be for the shepherds of Israel who feed only themselves! Why don't the shepherds feed the flock? You eat the milk curds from the sheep. You clothe yourselves with the wool from the sheep. You kill the fat sheep. But you do not feed the flock. You have not made the weak strong. You have not healed the sick. You have not put bandages on those that were hurt. You have not brought back those who strayed away. You have not searched for the lost. You ruled the sheep with cruel force. The sheep were scattered because there was no shepherd. Then they became food for every wild animal. My flock wandered over all the mountains and on every high hill. They were scattered over all the face of the earth. And no one searched or looked for them.

So, you shepherds, hear the word of the Lord. This is what the Lord God says: As surely as I live, my flock has been caught. It has become food for all the wild animals. This is because the flock has no shepherd. The shepherds did not search for my flock. No, they fed themselves instead of my flock. So, you shepherds, hear the word of the Lord. This is what the Lord God says: I am against the shepherds. I will blame them for what has happened to my sheep. I will not let them tend the flock anymore. Then the shepherds will stop feeding themselves. And I will take my flock from their mouths. My sheep will no longer be their food (EB).

Despite his desire to be a "good shepherd" in the eyes of God, Dobson draws a steady stream of fire from his constituency. Even at a rate of two negative letters per thousand, that means he receives more than four hundred written comments every month from people who are upset about something. Some offer constructive criticism. Others take off his hide. Ask yourself how you would cope with a similar situation in your line of work. Suppose a courier dropped by your house at the end of each month to tell you why four hundred people, whom you had attempted to serve, thought you were pompous, dishonest, stupid—or worst, heretical. Dobson receives this painful report every thirty days, which gives him that kind of bad news straight out of the gun barrel. The Correspondence Department, which prepares the report, has appropriately titled it "The Big Bomber Review."

Although this report contains as many as forty or fifty paragraphs excerpted from actual letters, Dobson reads each of them carefully. I have seen him change ministry policy or adjust a viewpoint as the result of a single letter. For example, I recall a response we received a few years ago from a woman who complained that many of the people pictured in our magazine appeared to be nearly perfect. "Why don't you occasionally photograph mothers who are overweight or a little plain?" she challenged. "You are perpetuating the myth that only beautiful people matter."

The simple answer was that we obtained most of our photos from stock agencies, which represent various photographers. Their inventories simply do not include pictures of average men and women. Nevertheless, Dobson asked us to *find* photographs of "ordinary" people, on the basis of this one comment out of 150,000 letters arriving that month. He obviously agrees with one of his favorite authors, William Manchester, who wrote, "Criticism serves the same function as pain in the human body. It may make us uncomfortable, but it draws our attention to a diseased state in our system."

As an example, the following statements, taken from a recent criticism report, are typical of the comments Dobson reads each month:

1. I was shocked that you, of all people, would blame the women's movement for devaluing the role of wife and mother. I was shocked because you, as a fighter against pornography, should know that Hugh Hefner and the *Playboy* phenomenon predate the women's movement, and could be more logically blamed for the diminished respect accorded homemakers. As the wife of a pastor, I am also frequently distressed to hear women say, "The church oppresses women. It supports male domination of women." Let us confess our own sins before we judge the women's movement.

2. Please do not send me any more "slick" envelopes. I do not doubt the sincerity of your message inside. But I do continue to need to let

you know the way your mailing is being received. In my spirit, it reflects neither the Lord nor the humble man I think that you are. Would you want me to send you a letter enclosed in an envelope with a wallet size photo of me taped on the front? I'm sorely tempted! Who are you promoting? James Dobson or Jesus? Please look again at your mailings and how they are promoted!

3. Thanks for all the good, helpful programs. One thing I might mention, as a homemaker and grandmother, in recent months my listening and enjoyment has somewhat decreased because of the (in my opinion) overemphasis on political and abortion issues. I am totally against abortion and realize it is a needed area of exposure, but personally it's getting a bit wearisome. I really don't mean this to be a put-down but thought you might like to hear one person's reason for not so diligently trying to never miss a program, as I once did.

4. Yesterday I sat at my desk preparing to write a letter of protest about a particular article in *Clubhouse* magazine. My husband and I are horrified that your organization, which we normally agree with, would exalt a young, immature Christian girl as a role model in *Clubhouse!* I am disappointed and ashamed that Focus has included this feature, which reeks of *Seventeen* magazine stories. Please remember that when we hold peers up to our children, very often there is little they truly benefit from. My daughter and son (eight and ten) both recognized the caliber of "Christianity" she represents, and our entire family agrees that she looks and acts like she is wholly sold on herself, not Christ. Please, if you include features on people, let them be mature Christians (Hudson Taylor, Amy Carmichael, Fanny Crosby, etc.) who have proved themselves faithful.

After reading the accumulated responses of his critics each month, Dobson says he feels as though he has been hit with a two-by-four about four hundred times. The most painful criticism, of course, is that which we recognize as valid indicators of ministry weaknesses.

I asked him if we could pose some of these more common and substantive criticisms to him. Dobson agreed, and I posed the following issues for his response.

Q. You were criticized in an article in *Christianity Today* magazine for the way you confront people who have failed to meet your high standards. You've gained a

reputation as someone who can be unduly harsh on certain occasions. How do you plead?

A. Guilty, your honor. I think I have made big improvements in this area because the Lord has demanded it. Still, I have to check myself when I am irritated. My tendency is to put my thoughts in writing, and that is what I must learn not to do. Let me explain.

I am a writer. I've always expressed my thoughts best in written language. Even when I was ten years old, I would write letters to my parents if I thought they had disciplined me unfairly. I much preferred to make my case on paper than face to face.

Through the years, therefore, my first reaction when I was irritated was to express that sentiment in writing. It was not until about 1981 that I began to see the disadvantages of that approach. There are many. First, when words are put on paper, their intensity does not diminish with the passage of time. There in the files, or at home in a spouse's possession, is a fiery message that carries its original impact even years after everyone has forgotten the issue that motivated it. When angry thoughts are expressed in black and white, they remain alive and dangerous—like an armed pipe bomb!

Second, there is something powerful about the written language. Remember that Jesus identified Himself entirely with the Scriptures: "In the beginning was the Word, and the Word was with God, and the Word was God" (John 1:1). Even the words of man can be a two-edged sword that cuts the soul to the quick. Harsh *spoken* words can also be destructive, of course, but they can't compare to those that are carefully arranged on paper and served up piping hot!

Third, I found at Focus on the Family that my tendency to put my reprimands in writing set the stage for other members of my staff to do the same. They began criticizing one another in memo-form, which brought immediate retaliation and countercharges. I quickly realized this was *wrong*.

Fourth, I found that my face to face encounters with those who needed correcting were not nearly so severe or painful. Sometimes the person was able to give me a logical explanation I hadn't considered. On other occasions, I saw vulnerability in his or her eyes that softened my own irritation.

What I'm telling you is that the Lord began talking to me about this entire area, and I feel I have mellowed significantly in recent years. But the criticism you mentioned, Rolf, has certainly been valid in times past. I was never capricious or vicious to people as a matter of course. Most of my strong memos went to those who had deliberately or slovenly failed to meet a need or follow a well-known policy. I have never been a tyrant to work for. Still, I needed to make some significant changes in the way I related to my colleagues—and I've attempted to do just that.

Q. **I suppose your tendency to be tough, especially in writing, would apply to your relationship with business associates, too.**

A. It sure would. I have actually gone back to the publishers of some of my early books and asked for forgiveness for the things I demanded of them. I'll never forget the time when my second book, *Hide or Seek*, came out. It arrived on the heels of *Dare to Discipline*, which had been enormously successful. I did not want to be a flash in the pan—a one-book author—who had nothing else of importance to say. As a result, I felt a great deal of pressure to produce another best seller. It was carnal pride, pure and simple. Then for some reason, I found *Hide or Seek* difficult to write, and I bogged down for two years in the process. It is probably my favorite book now, but I went through a tough time giving birth to it. When the book finally came off the press, I was one uptight young author. I was determined to make it go, or else. I went to New York City in 1974 and participated in seventeen radio, television, and newspaper interviews within a span of only three days. No price was too great to let the world know the book was available.

Shortly thereafter, Ernie Owen came to see me at Children's Hospital. He was my publisher from Fleming H. Revell in New Jersey. We went to eat together, and I gave him fits all during lunch.

"How come I can't find copies of *Hide or Seek* in the Christian bookstores?" I asked. "Where are you advertising the book, and why are you not keeping me informed of your plans?" On and on I went. Then suddenly, the man who is now my good friend, fired his own shots back at me.

"I want to know something about you," Ernie said. "How come this book is so important to you? Why are you acting like this? Why are you so uptight about the job we are doing?"

Ernie probably didn't know it at the time, but his responses made me very angry. Instead of doing his job as my representative, he was being rude to me and making me feel foolish for insisting on quality work from my publishers.

I quickly finished eating, shook hands with Ernie, and headed back across the street to the hospital. I got about fifty yards from the restaurant, when the Lord spoke to me. It was not an audible voice, but it was unmistakably *His*!

He said, "Son, those questions that Ernie was asking you a few minutes ago did not originate with him. They came from Me! *I* also want to know why you are pushing and shoving everyone so hard. Tell me why you're trying to force this book to be a success. Don't you know that you have *nothing* that I haven't given you, and that *Hide or Seek* will be successful *only* if I choose to bless it? So why are you trying to promote it on your own?"

If you have ever been "spanked" by the Lord, you know it is an unpleasant experience. I felt about three feet high.

"I understand, Lord," I said, and released *Hide or Seek* into His hands. "It is Yours. If You can use it, that's fine, and if not, I surrender my personal ambitions."

Hide or Seek took off like a rocket that month and is still selling well fifteen years later.

My point is that I am an intense person with strong opinions about how things ought to be done. I was especially that way when I was younger. I also had a pretty powerful temper in those days. But the Lord is beating those characteristics out of me. If I can live another hundred years, I may turn out to be a pretty nice guy.

Q. Speaking of *Hide or Seek*, that book is about building self-esteem in children. You have been criticized in recent years for being the guru of self-esteem, which some of your critics consider to be unbiblical.

A. Yes, I am aware of their criticism, and some of it appears deliberately designed to distort my beliefs and teachings. If I am *anything*, I am an orthodox, mainline evangelical in my thought and writings. I would never do or say anything I felt was contradictory to Scripture. And yet, being a psychologist, I am an easy mark for those who want to describe me as some kind of heretic. My views on self-esteem are sometimes offered as the best case in point. Let me explain what I think about that subject, and then people can judge the validity of my opinions for themselves.

We have come through an era in Western thought that was characterized by extreme "me-ism." The personhood of the self became primary, and nothing mattered but self-aggrandizement, self-fulfillment, and self-gratification. That entire movement had a foul aroma to it, and it was fully contradictory to the Scriptures, which command believers to deny themselves, to take up their crosses, and to follow Jesus. God clearly hates haughtiness, independence, selfishness, and pride. One cannot read the Bible without understanding that fact.

Incredibly, however, several Christian authors and speakers now make a decent living by going around the country telling people that I believe and promote this kind of humanistic psychobabble. Heaven help us! My book *Hide or Seek*, which has been singled out as an example of this heresy, relates not to me-ism at all, but to the protection of a child's emotional apparatus during the particularly vulnerable years of his development. Rather than recommending the elevation of ourselves, I was trying in that book to help parents protect their children from the epidemic of self-hatred that has besieged an entire generation of young people.

Here is the frame of reference for *Hide or Seek*: I've dealt with so many teenagers like the girl I'll call Tracy. She is fourteen years old and weighs eighty-eight pounds soaking wet. She is covered with pimples and blackheads, and her teeth point simultaneously in four directions. Her hair is stringy and straight, and she shuffles when she walks. Every day of her life she is mocked, rejected, ignored, and hated by her peers. They laugh when she passes in the hall. Her unofficial name at school is "Witchnose." Her parents are also products of the system that values physical attractiveness, and they treat her with the same disdain as her peers. This poor child (and the millions like her) is so crushed by life that she cannot look another person in the eye. She slinks through her day, weeping in school restrooms and sitting at home alone on Saturday nights. If there is one thing this brokenhearted kid needs, it is a friend . . . someone who would say, "I understand; I care; I love you and God loves you." She also needs a book like *Hide or Seek* that will tell her parents about her pain and will offer some suggestions for reducing it.

What she doesn't need is a noncaring biblical analysis from a person who has never counseled such a kid in his life, saying that God prefers humiliation to adequacy. I don't believe it. Tens of thousands of these teenagers are killing themselves every year because they can see no reason to go on living. Others sink into drug abuse, sexual immorality, and crime. The common denominator among them is a personal revulsion that goes to the very core of their being. And for the life of me, I can't see how it can be considered "unbiblical" to try to protect them from a social system that perpetuates this hatred!

In one of the most absurd statements made on this subject to date, one writer has said with a straight face, "Low self-esteem does not exist. It is a myth. The real problem is a matter of disguised pride. The self-concept is not too low, in these cases—it is too high." Listen carefully, now, to the implications of this statement. If there is no such thing as low self-esteem—no condition known as self-hatred—no overwhelming feelings of inadequacy and inferiority—then it stands to reason that a child cannot be damaged by the stressful experiences of childhood. If there are no wounded spirits and damaged egos, it is impossible to hurt a child emotionally.

He is impervious to alcoholic parents or abusing adults who tell him he is ugly, unwanted, unloved, and destined to fail in everything he does. When the pedophile strips a boy or girl naked and photographs them with pistols or mouse-traps on the body, it does not damage their self-esteem! When unwanted kids are bounced from one rejecting home to another, it does not affect their self-concept! When an adolescent is laughed at every day of his life and is never invited or included or respected, it only serves to inflate his ego! The only problem is that such a person is puffed up with concealed pride! That is pure nonsense, and I'm pleased that very few people seem to believe it.

We read in Ps. 103:13, "As a father pitieth his children, so the Lord pitieth them that fear Him." *That* is the tenderness with which the Heavenly Father approaches wounded, pathetic human beings who have been shredded by life. Thank goodness, *He* knows the difference between a broken spirit and haughty self-sufficiency.

Q. Another common criticism of the Focus on the Family ministry is that it is geared only to white, middle, or upper-class families who know nothing of the problems of the poor. Is that valid?

A. It *was* valid in the early years. I was the primary spokesman on the radio, and naturally, I talked from my own experiences. Not coming from a minority family or one that experienced extreme poverty, I had a blind spot that quickly began to show up. However, as this was pointed out to me and I saw the accuracy of the criticism, we began to change our approach. If you listen to our programming today, you'll hear broadcasts aimed at single-parent families, inner-city and minority families, and those who struggle financially. Furthermore, we help support the ministry of Dr. Tony Evans, a brilliant black pastor who has a great burden for inner-city families. More recently, we have begun a Spanish version of *Focus on the Family* (*Enfoque al la Familia*), which is rapidly spreading into Hispanic homes. Our magazines often feature photographs of black and Hispanic individuals, and we regularly invite members of minority groups to be guests on the broadcasts. In short, we are trying hard to address the criticism you mention, but I believe we still have room for improvement.

Q. You are sometimes accused of being a chauvinist—of giving men a higher place in society than women. Are they equal in God's sight or not?

A. I fully affirm the equality of the sexes and their personhood and value in the sight of God. I do not believe, however, this implies equivalence of office or function. The Bible clearly distinguishes between male and female roles within the marital bond—though this should not be taken to mean that one partner is more important than or superior to the other. Instead, functioning together in a complementary relationship of mutual submission, the Christian husband and wife become, as is taught in the book of Ephesians, a reflection of the love that exists between Christ and His Church.

At this point, however, I want to issue a warning. The scriptural pathway here is narrow, and it is easy to fall into twin errors on either side of the road. The first is that of promoting male dominance and female repression. Yes, I believe the Bible makes it clear that a man should bear the responsibility for leadership in the home. But it is only as a leader that his wife is asked to submit to him (Eph. 5:22), not as a tyrant or superior being. She is not disenfranchised or robbed of her personhood by his leadership, nor is he given the right to run roughshod over her opinions and feelings. Rather, he is to love and cherish her—and to die for her if necessary—even as Christ loved the Church (Eph. 5:25). I believe he should include her in the process of reaching mutually satisfactory decisions, always working to incorporate her perspectives and opinions, and seeking compromise whenever necessary. In those situations where they simply cannot find common ground, I believe the Scripture gives the man the prerogative—and responsibility—to choose and direct. But this does not mean he is free to disregard the needs and feelings of his partner. Rather, he must in this case be more sensitive and considerate than ever, bearing in mind that he will ultimately answer to God not only for his choices, but for his treatment of his wife. First Peter 3:7 even says a man's prayers will not be answered if he treats his wife disrespectfully.

The second pitfall we must avoid is equally dangerous. With the current sensitivity to male chauvinism and authoritarianism, it would be easy to disregard the concept of masculine leadership altogether. In reacting against abuses and misuses of authority, we must be careful not to throw the baby out with the bathwater. In my opinion, the breakdown of many families today is due in part to the failure of men to assume their God-given responsibilities. If, in an attempt to avoid male domination, we swing to the other extreme and strip husbands of their ability to lead, we will be disregarding God's plan for marriage and the family, and will ultimately court social disaster.

Q. **You have given so much attention to the home schooling movement on your broadcasts. Why do you seem to advocate this unconventional option of education over others?**

A. That is a misrepresentation of my position. I recognize that a strong diversity of opinions exists regarding the various educational options now available to families. I contend that no one choice is the best for every child. Rather, I feel that parents should consider all three alternatives—home schooling, private Christian schools, and public schools—in light of their particular set of circumstances before reaching any final decisions. In keeping with this perspective, I have attempted to balance our programming to include discussions of each of these three educational formats.

Unfortunately, some people mistakenly feel that when we feature a broadcast on one of the alternatives, we are somehow making a critical judgment about the other two. Others have been negative of my inclusive position, arguing that one particular educational form should be emphasized exclusively. Not all parents are cut out to be home educators, for instance. For other families, Christian education may not be possible because of prohibitive costs or distances. Humanistic teachings may be a problem in local public schools. I feel parents should review carefully the relevant issues in their situation and then make the best choice for their child. My role has been to assist in this process by illuminating the options.

Q. There are those who think your position on abortion is extreme because you wouldn't even permit it in cases of incest, rape, or where the child is defective. How do you justify such a position?

A. Only in rare instances when the life of the mother is literally at stake do I feel we have the moral authority to destroy a developing fetus. My reasoning is based on this simple question: Is there any fundamental difference between a baby who resides in his mother's uterus and one who has made an eight-inch journey down the birth canal? If so, what is the difference? At what point in the birth process does God's mantle of humanness fall upon an individual? Is there anything particularly mystical about the expulsion from the mother's body that could account for a transformation from mere protoplasm to a human being with an eternal soul? I think not. Surely the Lord does not look upon the baby inside the uterus with any less love and concern than one who enters the world a few minutes later. The only difference between them is that one can be seen and the other cannot.

If that premise can be accepted, then it is equally immoral to kill either those born or those yet to be born. Physical and intellectual health and the nature of conception are irrelevant to the issue. Even most proabortionists would not propose that we destroy children arriving in the delivery room with unexpected deficiencies. Indeed, the authorities would charge them with murder for killing a neonate who lacked adequate cognitive function or who had only a few weeks to live. We would be obligated morally and legally to let nature take its course, regardless of the severity of the baby's condition. Likewise, we would not kill a one-day-old infant who was conceived in a rape or an incident of incest.

Once born, the deliberate destruction of life is unthinkable. Why, then, is such a baby considered "fair game" when he resides within his mother's uterus? It is true that the law recognizes a different status for those born versus those unborn, but the law in this instance is wrong. There is no biological or moral basis for the distinction. Infanticide merely *seems* acceptable when we don't have to witness the death process of a tiny victim we have not yet met.

Therefore, all the arguments in favor of terminating the defective or handicapped unborn child must be weighed against this understanding, including "he's going to die anyway," "he'll only suffer if we let him live," "his life will only bring pain to his parents," "he has no chance of living a normal life," and "this is really the best way out for everyone concerned." When applied to the baby who has managed to limp into this world, the evil of these rationalizations becomes apparent. *No* justification will permit us to give a newborn a lethal injection of cyanide. But hours earlier when the mother's contractions have not yet begun, some would feel righteously justified in tearing the same defective or ill-conceived infant to pieces. The proposition is categorically immoral in my view.

In conclusion, allow me to add a footnote about the criticism to which Dr. Dobson is regularly subjected. Most of the concerns, like those on the previous pages, are valid and help him to improve his outreach to families. But occasionally, the rebukes are completely unfounded and somewhat amusing. I remember one gentleman who condemned Dobson as a racist because he mentioned the Black Plague during a broadcast. Apparently, the critic was unfamiliar with this common reference to history's worst epidemic, which swept Europe in the fifteenth century.

People will also criticize Dobson over the most trivial matters. One irate woman expressed her anger about a Dobson family portrait published in the *Focus on the Family* magazine. She was livid because the photo showed the Dobsons' pet dog sitting on the couch. In her opinion, Dr. Dobson was a poor role model for allowing a canine on the sofa.

I asked Dr. Dobson what kind of criticism bothered him the most. He said in reply, "There are only two comments that tend to get under my skin. The first is that I've become too big for my britches—too high and mighty for my own good—that I run over the less powerful and crush those who get in my way. Naturally, I suppose, I believe such a criticism is unfounded. In fact, we often make decisions at Focus on the Family that are not in the best interests of the ministry because we want to be certain not to misuse the influence God has loaned us. I *despise* haughty pride, and that's why it offends me when someone alleges that we are consumed by our self-anointed importance. I *know* how inadequate I am for the assignment God has given me.

"Second, it hurts me when someone charges me with being unbiblical. I care about the Word more than my own life, and I would never intentionally do anything to contradict it. The Scriptures *do* have to be interpreted, of course, and some passages are subject to differing understandings. Thus, I wish my detractors would say they differ with my *interpretations* of Scripture instead of implying that I have willingly disregarded or disrespected the Scriptures."

These kinds of criticism reflect the intimate nature of Dr. Dobson's daily radio program. His listeners relate to him as though he were a member of their own families. Thus, when he disappoints them, they let him have it with both barrels! For Dobson, living in the limelight must feel at times more like living under a heat lamp.

9

The Great Awakening

One of the most common criticisms of James Dobson these days is that he is becoming "too political"—that he has politicized Focus on the Family's ministry to parents and children. Other critics have even alleged that he is positioning himself to run for the presidency, a notion he finds amusing.

"There are only five reasons why that rumor is unfounded," he quips. "First, I don't want the job. Second, God wouldn't let me have the job. Third, I'm unqualified for the job. Fourth, I couldn't get elected, and fifth, Shirley would leave me if I tried. Other than that, it's a great idea."

Dobson also feels that the criticism of his efforts to influence public policy is based largely on misinformation. First, he has *always* been concerned about the social environment and its relevance to the family. This emphasis can be found in his first book, *Dare to Discipline*. Throughout its pages, which were written twenty years ago, you can find his views about the political climate in which children were being raised. He has not just suddenly become concerned about that matter.

Furthermore, Dobson has not significantly increased the percentage of Focus on the Family's investment in public policy. Yes, he has opened a Washington office, and the ministry does produce a widely circulated magazine called *Citizen*. The ministry is also attempting to develop statewide coalitions in the battle to save the family. But, in context, *every* department and program at

140

Focus has grown through the years. Relatively speaking, the public policy effort is still in balance with the other areas of emphasis. Less than 1 percent of the 1989 budget was spent in lobbying activity, and only 6 percent was targeted for all aspects of government involvement.

Finally, Dr. Dobson's participation in public policy is regulated by a series of very strict and well-defined policies, which he never violates. These are the official guidelines, which were adopted by the Board of Directors:

1. He never endorses any political candidates or publicly supports or opposes any politician by name.

2. He never engages in partisan politics. He has no great admiration for either the Democratic or Republican parties per se, and he is not identified as a supporter of either one.

3. He has absolutely no political ambitions personally. He has not been and never will be a candidate for public office.

4. He never addresses political issues that are unrelated to the family, such as defense policy, foreign relations, or the economy.

Why then does Dobson bother with public policy at all? This controversial activity is dangerous to the long-term interests of the ministry and could just as well be skirted. Even as I write, the *Washington Post* is preparing a personality profile of Dobson that will undoubtedly be critical in tone. So why not simply tiptoe away and deal only with the "safer" issues, such as raising children and making the most of married life?

The reason Dobson attempts to influence and monitor public policy is because he believes the foundations of the family are being systematically destroyed. Many people in society believe this institution has outlived its usefulness and should be buried. Others want to twist and modify it to fit their humanistic values. For more than twenty years, therefore, the institution of the family has been subjected to an endless array of bad ideas, including the sexual revolution, open marriage, no-fault divorce laws, devastating taxes, hostility to children, abortion on demand, ridicule of homemakers, war between the sexes, and the plague of obscenity.

James Dobson became involved in public policy because the family needed to be defended from those who disrespected its heritage and the value system upon which it rests. At one time it was protected in the United States by our representatives in Congress who shared our Judeo-Christian understanding. But that day is past. Now this wonderful institution is caught in a massive tug-of-war between competing special-interest groups. The winner of that contest will not only set the agenda for families in the foreseeable future but will capture the biggest prize of all—the hearts and minds of our children. The stakes are simply too high to walk away from the table.

But there is another reason Dr. Dobson participates in the public policy arena. Not only does the family need to be *defended*, but it needs to be *represented* in government. Historically, the institutions of marriage and parenthood have had no lobbying support in the nation's capital—a city where virtually every special-interest group has a presence. In fact, the third largest employer in Washington, D.C., after government and tourism, is the "Associations" industry. More than 3,200 national associations have their headquarters in the capital for the express purpose of furthering their causes.

Did you know, for example, that the Possum Growers and Breeders have an office in Washington? Other groups represented there include the National Paint, Varnish and Lacquer Association; the American Association of Sex Educators, Counselors and Therapists; the American Baseball Fans Association; and the Confederate Memorial Association. Of course, liberal groups like Planned Parenthood, NOW, the ACLU, and Gay Partners are also present in Washington to monitor legislation, conduct research, lobby Congress, and form political action groups.

Given that competition, how can we expect the millions of uninformed and unrepresented families around the United States to be given a fair shake in Washington? We can't and they aren't! Look at the tax code, for example. In 1948 a family of four at the median income paid almost no federal tax. Today, a similar family works several months of each year just for the IRS. Then if the family happens to live where there is a state income tax, they'll be dunned again. This is an example of a public policy decision that has operated against hard-working mothers and fathers for the past two decades. Since their interests have not been represented, millions of mothers who would like to stay at home and raise their children are now forced to seek formal employment. Someone should have been there to reflect their interests when lobbyists were successfully shifting the tax burden from corporations to individual families.

Seeing this great need for families to be defended and represented in government, the question should not be, "Why is Dobson becoming political?" but, "Why isn't everyone?"

I asked Dobson to return to the early days of Focus on the Family and tell us in his own words what lured him into the public arena. What did he see then that lit the fire that still burns in his soul today? This is his response:

I came of age professionally in a very troubled time, as you know. There were powerful social changes underway in those days that would rock the Western world for years to come. Chief among them, of course, was the Women's Liberation Movement. The feminists who created it and gave it definition had some good ideas in the beginning, including "equal pay for equal work" and the rights of women to be respected and taken seriously in the workplace. Congressmen and state legislators were quick to grasp this opportunity to impress 50 percent of the voters, and they rapidly translated many feminist ideas into law.

Heady with success and encouraged by an enthusiastic press, the *real* agenda of radical feminists then came into focus. They wanted the whole pie! They took to the streets, burned their bras, and declared war on men. (Gloria Steinem, one of the gurus of the movement, once wrote, "Women need men like fish need a bicycle.") The media were cheering widely by this time as feminists demanded civil rights for homosexuals, unrestricted access to abortions at government expense, and federally sponsored child-care centers to liberate women from the burden of mothering. Every vestige of the Judeo-Christian ethic was assaulted during that era, despite its long history as the culture's central repository of values.

Even the English language was quickly modified during that time to eliminate its "sexist" terminology. Phyllis Schlafly, writing in her book *The Power of the Christian Woman,* described how feminists

143

pressured Macmillan Publishing Company to introduce sex-neutral language in all of its textbooks. A guideline was written to teach editors a new vocabulary:

> Henceforth, you may not say mankind, it should be humanity. You may not say brotherhood, it should be amity. Manpower must be replaced by human energy; forefathers should give way to precursors. Chairman and salesman are out; and chairperson and salesperson are in.
>
> Males must be shown wearing aprons just as often as females. Fathers should be pictured doing household chores and nursing a sick child, mother working at her desk while dad clears the dining room table, little girls reaching toward snakes instead of recoiling from them, boys crying or preening in front of a mirror and fathers using hair spray.

As the feminists' campaign to reshape Western society gathered momentum, it became obvious that one major barrier stood in their way. The big problem, they decided, was the institution of the family. Traditional marriages and parenthood were the oppressors that had enslaved women and crushed their spirits for centuries. No doubt about it. The family had to go.

Actress Shirley MacLaine was one of the leaders of that charge, as she is today with her New Age concepts. This confused woman has apparently convinced millions of gullible believers that inanimate crystals can bring good luck and release the powers of the universe. She was saying equally unfounded things nineteen years ago. *Look* magazine quoted MacLaine as she fired a salvo at the family and the Christian concept of fidelity in marriage:

> All this goes back as far as Christian culture, to what Mary and Joseph started. You know it's just a million things that have been handed down with the Christian ethic, so when you begin to question the family, you have to question all those things.
>
> I don't think it's desirable to conform to having one mate and for those two people to raise children. But everyone believes that's the ideal. They go around frustrated most of their lives because they can't find one mate. But who said that's the natural basic personality of man? To whom does monogamy make sense? Then why should they adhere to this state of monogamy? In a democratic family, individuals understand their natural tendencies, bring them out in the open, discuss them, and very likely follow them. And these tendencies are definitely not monogamous.

How's that for sheer wisdom in a time of moral crisis? MacLaine thought the world would be a much better place if we could just have more adultery among married couples and a lot less of this stuff that—you know—Mary and Joseph started a long time ago. Bless her heart, I've read some strange ideas in my lifetime but Shirley's views are in a class by themselves.

She was not alone in the early 1970s, of course. Consider the following quotations from that era that tell us where the movement was headed. There can be little doubt about the intended target!

Marriage has existed for the benefit of men and has been a legally sanctioned method of control over women . . . the end of the institution of marriage is a necessary condition for the liberation of women. Therefore, it is important for us to encourage women to leave their husbands and not live individually with men . . . we must work to destroy it (marriage). (*The Document, Declaration of Feminism*)

We really don't know how to raise children . . . the fact that children are raised in families means there's no equality . . . in order to raise children with equality, we must take them away from families and raise them . . . (Dr. Mary Jo Bane, *Tulsa World* newspaper, August 21, 1977, AP wire)

By the year 2000 we will, I hope, raise our children to believe in human potential, not God. (Gloria Steinem)

No deity will save us; we must save ourselves. Promises of immortal salvation or fear of eternal damnation are both illusory and harmful. (*Humanist Manifesto II*, signed by Betty Friedan, founder of National Organization for Women)

All of history must be rewritten in terms of the oppression of women. We must go back to ancient female religions (like witchcraft) . . . (*The Document, Declaration of Feminism*)

NOW (National Organization for Women) endorses . . . widespread sex education, provision of birth control information and contraceptives, the repeal of all laws restricting abortion, contraception and sexual activity between consenting adults in private. (*Revolution: Tomorrow is NOW*, Handbook for the National Organization for Women)

. . . the new liberated woman of 1970 is not an old battle-ax. Well-educated, privileged, she is often attractive and almost always young . . . she is, in addition, idealistic, intense . . . and she is furious. She has nothing against premarital sex and has usually tried it. It's just that she finds it disappointing at best, not worth the trouble (isn't it easier to masturbate?) . . . she wants

to reform sex practices in line with sex experiments . . . Bad
language is a way of proving you're not a lady, so liberated
women may toss off . . . four-letter words from which men ex-
tract a sexual thrill. (Caroline Bird, *Born Female*, 1970)

Let me ask you, the reader, a delicate question about this period in
Western history. Where were you when the Christian concept of marital fidelity, lifelong love, commitment to the welfare of children, protection for the unborn child and two thousand years of family tradition
first came under fire? Perhaps you were asleep with the rest of the
Christian community. We all dozed throughout the early 1970s when
the foundations of society were being undermined. We were still snor-
ing in 1973 when the United States Supreme Court issued its infamous
Roe v. Wade decision that permitted 25 million American babies to be
murdered. Who knows how great the number of slaughtered children
has been worldwide?

What is tragic and yet curious about that period between 1965 and
1975 is that the radical left had virtually no organized opposition. The
media were entirely sympathetic to its point of view. It raised up
brilliant champions like Phil Donahue who crushed anyone who tried
to disagree. They even had a strange kind of mystical power over the
old, mainline Christian denominations.

In an article in *Time* magazine that I will never forget (Dec. 13,
1971), the mainline Christian denominations were reportedly leaning
toward a redefinition of immorality. The United Methodist Church
had just received a resolution from its Committee on Family Life that
condoned sex for single persons, homosexuals, and those living in
"other styles of interpersonal relationships." The Presbyterian Church
had also received a report on sexual behavior from its twelve-member
Task Force of Church Professionals. Quoting from that statement,
"it suggests that the arbitrary requirement of premarital virginity be
replaced by a sliding scale of allowable premarital sex, geared to the
permanence, depth, and maturity of the relationship." The task force
said there were "exceptional circumstances" in which adultery might
be justified. It also said the church should explore the possibility of
communal and other sex styles for the unmarried. The United Church
of Christ had just received its own authorized statement written by
six Christian education executives "which maintains that sex is moral
if the partners are committed to the fulfilling of each other's personhood"—pointedly omitting marriage as a prerequisite.

Time magazine summarized the shifting interpretations of morality
in this way: "To the many laymen who are already making up their

own minds about sex, the new approach to ethics may seem irrelevant or at best a trendy attempt by the churches to be 'with it' in a society that is adopting increasingly permissive sexual rules."

While I have never been one to throw my theological understandings and beliefs at others, I can tell you I was angry at the mainline churches for their flirtation with evil. I knew it was wrong then. The world knows it today, with perhaps 10 million people around the globe facing death from AIDS, and thirty-eight sexually transmitted diseases running rampant through human society. God's old-fashioned idea of morality doesn't seem so out-of-date from this perspective.

I'll also admit that during this period of my life I was exasperated by what I saw happening. There we were, steadily losing everything I cared about—everything I believed in—and yet so many of my countrymen seemed not to notice. Every month, Hugh Hefner took another swipe at Christianity, at morality, and at the family in his "Playboy Philosophy, Part 36," yet I never heard *one* sermon in response to him through all those years. The big theme in churches then, both evangelical and mainline, was positive thinking and the great love of God. We sat in Sunday services for ten years and heard ministers tell us how to tap into the power of the Almighty to achieve health, wealth, and happiness. All we had to do was make the right noises to Him. He was a big genie in a bottle ready to serve the materialistic desires of a self-contented society. Oral Roberts' choir was singing his theme song on television each week, "Something good is going to happen to you."

Sitting in pews near me in my church were the people I was counseling. I knew the sordid things they were doing from Monday to Saturday. I could identify the active gays. I knew the adulterers. I had talked to the dishonest businessmen and to the mother who aborted her baby and to the college kids who were "shacking up." Where, I wondered, was the call to repentance? Where was mention of the terrible judgment of God upon those who willfully wallowed in sin and filth? And speaking of sin, whatever happened to that biblical word? It just fell out of our vocabulary during that unbelievable decade.

Even if a timorous pastor *did* mention the forbidden word, it was spoken with no conviction and no passion. Preachers quit "preaching" to us. They began "sharing" with us. That became the cliché of the period. "I just want to share a few ideas with you this morning," they would say.

"Come on, man!" I thought. "The world is going to hell, and you're planning to share some watery soup with us? Don't you have anything of importance to tell us from the Word of God? Doesn't the Scripture speak emphatically about a perverse and evil generation that has forgotten the Lord and trampled underfoot His holy commandments?" I'll tell you truthfully, I gnawed my tongue for a decade, and I'm still not sure we have it right.

The year 1977 was to be the darkest for me personally. We had reached the apex of the feminist movement and the radical ideas they represented. That entire movement would soon begin to fizzle, but no one knew it then. Certainly the politicians did not know that a conservative backlash was coming. The previous year, President Gerald Ford had proclaimed the following twelve months as an "International Women's Year." His wife Betty was a fervent supporter of "the movement" and undoubtedly urged him to get on the bandwagon. He did. In 1976 the president appointed a special commission comprised entirely of feminists and gave them $300,000 in government funds. The new commission promptly lobbied Congress for an additional $5 million to finance conferences in every state throughout 1977. Then they proposed to conclude with a huge convention at the end of the year. By that time, President Jimmy Carter was in the White House. His wife Rosalynn was also a vigorous supporter of the Equal Rights Amendment (ERA) and the feminist cause, so away we went.

The International Women's Conference was held in Houston, Texas, and it was a feminist's dream. Staged to present a massive rally on behalf of ERA, it was controlled entirely by the ladies of the left. Only those with the philosophy of Bella Abzug, Gloria Steinem, and Betty Friedan were permitted to participate, even though the event was funded by every taxpayer's money. The rest of American womankind sat at home and watched on television.

For an entire week, the media showcased this conference as though it were a party convention during a presidential election year. The event became a coronation for the National Organization for Women and the gender-free society it envisioned. As predictably as night follows day, the delegates recommended overwhelmingly that abortion rights be extended at government expense, that gay and lesbian rights be secured, that federalized child-care centers be developed, that the Equal Rights Amendment be passed, and the rest of the feminist agenda be implemented. The world press was turning cartwheels. They ran with the message and shouted it from the rooftops to everyone who would listen.

What a coup this was for those who hoped to redesign society—a society without families—a society without the moral hang-ups of the past. But in the darkness of that hour, something encouraging and totally unpredictable was happening. Sitting at home watching on television were millions of women who were saying, "Hey! What's going on? I don't agree with what those women are saying! Where are the delegates who believe in marriage and the traditional family? What is this gay and lesbian stuff? How did all that federal money get funneled into the hands of such radical people? Why isn't *my* point of view represented?"

Of course, we didn't know then that this reaction was taking place around the United States. But we sure know it now. Those irritated wives and homemakers became the army that Phyllis Schlafly mobilized to stop the ERA dead in its tracks. You talk about a modern day story of David and Goliath. Mrs. Schlafly took on the power structure of the entire country and stopped it cold.

Arrayed against her were the president and past president of the United States, their first ladies, the majority of Congress, the majority of the Senate, the most glamorous men and women in Hollywood, the majority of American newspapers, the editorial writers of all the major radio and television networks, all the prominent news anchors from Walter "That's the Way It Is" Cronkite to Barbara Walters, the hosts of major television talk shows, including but not limited to the silver-haired Merv Griffin, and the not-yet-silver-haired Mr. Donahue, virtually all producers and directors of sitcom and dramatic television shows, the gay and lesbian movements—and, alas, the feminists. That armada of awesome might and power sailed proudly into battle against a single leaky rowboat in which an unarmed but rather angry woman sat.

Phyllis Schlafly, a lawyer by training and the mother of five, took on the armada and sank the entire fleet. She had very little money and the enthusiastic support of practically no one. No one, that is, except the majority of American women who had not yet burned their bras.

Thirty-five state legislatures had already passed the ERA when she got into the fight. Only three more were necessary to lock it into the Constitution, and they were practically leaning over the goal line. That's when Schlafly stepped out of the phone booth with a big red "S" on her chest. I watched her go eyeball to eyeball with Donahue, and she nailed him at his own game. She was intimidated by no one, and her instincts were correct. In winning that battle against the ERA, the steam began leaking from the balloon that carried the radical feminists to the skies.

Two years later, President Carter decided to stage an encore for the social engineers. He called it "The White House Conferences on the Family" and set the date for 1980. Millions of us must have been thinking to ourselves, "Not *this* time, Mr. President!"

True to form, only one Christian leader was invited to sit on the eleven-member planning commission for the White House Conferences. That is a ratio we have come to expect. Not knowing the vast number of my countrymen who felt the way I did, I began asking the administration to appoint me as a delegate to the event. It is the only time I have ever asked for a public appointment, but it was to no avail. I received a series of polite form letters from low-level bureaucrats explaining that my name would be given due consideration. I knew it was a brush-off. Sure enough, nearly a year went by, and no telegram arrived from the White House. Carter did not call. Rosalynn was silent.

By that time, our "Focus on the Family" radio program was being heard on about 150 stations, once each week. It was certainly not the widely heard broadcast it is today, but someone must have been listening. I simply mentioned on the air one day that I was very concerned about what had happened in Houston and that I would like to be a representative of the traditional family this time around. Then I expressed the same idea in a letter to our supporters.

To my utter shock, and to the dismay of President Carter's staff, 80,000 letters hit the White House in the next few days. I was later told that the volume of mail alarmed the decision makers there who had been busily planning another "Houston" type event.

After zigging and zagging for a few months, the conference administrators invited me to come to Washington, D.C. to participate in the Research Forum that *preceded* the White House Conferences. The idea was to bring in the university people—the professional community— to provide a research foundation for the three grass-roots conferences to follow. I spoke that night on the same program with the likes of Dr. Urie Bronfenbreuner, one of the foremost authorities in child development at that time. I had heard him speak eight years earlier in a conference in Miami, during which he said child-care centers would be extremely damaging to children. But on the big night in the nation's capital, he waffled. *No* man wanted to take on that angry bunch of women who screamed insults at every male who opposed them.

I spoke that evening on the things in which I believed, and received a polite but unenthusiastic response from the audience. Yet two interesting things happened that night. First, I was approached by President Carter's director of the White House Conferences, James Guy Tucker. He asked if he could buy me a Coke before taking me back to the hotel. I agreed, and we left together.

After we were seated in a restaurant, Tucker said, "I got your mail." I laughed. "Oh yeah?" I said.

"Yes. And it scared me," he continued. "I didn't want anyone with that kind of support being in an official position for the conferences. It could cause difficulties for us. But I listened carefully to what you had to say tonight, and I liked your point of view. I didn't agree with a lot of it, but I see where you're coming from."

Tucker and I continued talking for two hours, and then he made a statement that was to change my life. "I want to tell you something," he began. "I've been in Washington for a long time, and I know where the human resources can be found. If I need a liberal female with a Ph.D. for some assignment, I can find her in a minute. If I want to appoint a homosexual physician from a major medical school, I have names to choose from. But it's a fact that people like you cannot be found in this city. Those with university training from accredited institutions who also hold to traditional, profamily, Christian perspectives are *NOT* here. They have never been here, to my knowledge. To be honest, I didn't know that people like you existed until I got involved in these conferences and began to travel around the country. Then I found a few. But they do not participate in government!" .

How unfortunate in a representative form of government that is designed by the people and for the people that Christians have been taught to stay home and mind their own business. They have withheld their vital influence and ignored the critical issues of public policy. In so doing, they have forfeited their opportunities to shape their government and have turned over the key decisions by default to those who despise the Christian system of values. Yet that disengagement by Christians has been going on for decades.

Likewise, billions of dollars are doled out each year by the government in the form of federal grants awarded to recipients chosen by grant reviewers. Who are these gatekeepers for the public trust? They are, for the most part, extremely liberal, Eastern academics who wouldn't give a dime to a profamily advocate if their lives hung on it. But where are the Christian professionals who are willing to plow through a stack of boring grant applications to help direct those funds? They hardly exist. I made up my mind that night while talking to James Guy Tucker that I would do my best to change the lopsided representation in Washington.

Then the second happy development occurred that night in Washington, D.C. I met in a hotel room with eight other Christians attending the Research Forum, and we had a meaningful time of prayer on our knees. During the discussion that followed, we laid plans for what subsequently became the Family Research Council with Jerry Regier as its president. (Jerry was one of the men in the hotel room that night.) Gary Bauer, who was President Reagan's senior domestic policy advisor, now holds that FRC post. Recently, FRC has merged with Focus on the Family and is doing a fine job of representing the Christian perspective in government.

Oh yes! James Guy Tucker appointed me a few weeks later to be a delegate at the White House Conferences on the Family, and later, to be on the Task Force that summarized the findings. That's how I became involved in public policy. I've been in there slugging it out ever since. That's how it happened.

Let me make one last thing very clear. Washington, D.C. is one of the great power centers of the world. Most people who go there to work or to manipulate the system are attracted by the glamour of power and by the benefits of government influence. Whether or not your readers choose to believe it, our reasons for being in the capital are very different. We want nothing from our public policy efforts as individuals except the satisfaction of making a difference during a time of moral and familial crisis. That is its own reward.

What better proof of Dobson's avowed disinterest in politics than his rejection of the "plums" that have already come his way? He was asked during the early years of the Reagan administration if he would permit his name to be considered as commissioner of the Office of Children, Youth, and Families—a $400 million program within the Department of Health and Human Services. Seven years later, Dobson was approached on three occasions by the new Bush administration about the possibility of his becoming secretary of Health and Human Services. Acknowledging the honor of being considered, he did not permit himself to be a candidate in either instance. "God has put me where He wants me," he said to his friends. Those of us who work with him believe what he says. If he wanted high public office, he could have achieved it by now.

Dr. Dobson has, on the other hand, continued to exercise significant influence in Washington. He became a regular consultant to President Reagan during his eight years in office, sitting with him in the Cabinet Room or the Oval Office. A "Focus on the Family" radio broadcast was recorded with the president in the Oval Office, one of the few private interviews granted by Mr. Reagan during either term. Dr. Dobson also served as cochairman of the Citizens for Tax Reform at the president's request and then accepted the tougher assignments relating to juvenile delinquency, teen pregnancy, child abduction, and pornography.

When Dobson was honored at a banquet in Washington, D.C. during 1987, President Reagan prepared a videotaped message that included these words:

> Good evening, ladies and gentlemen. I'm delighted to be able to have a part in this tribute to that outstanding champion of the family and my friend, Jim Dobson.
>
> We've fought many battles together. We've known victory, and, yes, defeat, but he has always come through. I know I can depend on Jim Dobson and that loyal radio audience of Focus on the Family. In fact, I want to express my deep gratitude to you for serving on the attorney general's Commission on Pornography. I believe with you that the battle against pornography is a winnable war.
>
> Jim, you are certainly a worthy recipient of the first Marion Pfister Anschutz Award. I know of no one else who has been more courageous and effective as a defender and encourager of the family. The family is the oldest, most tested, and most reliable unit of society. It is divinely created and sustained. God has pronounced blessings upon the family throughout biblical history. The institution of the family is the guardian of our heritage. In fact, it is the only institution in all of human experience and history capable of producing responsible citizens for society.
>
> Yes, the family carries divine significance. And yet, there are those who are always tampering with its values and structure—when you and I know better. That's why I recently signed an Executive Order asking that all regulations and programs consider their impact on the family. [Dobson first suggested this idea to President Reagan in 1983.]
>
> This is a great night, not only for Jim Dobson, but for the family. Your gathering together for this occasion is a message to friends and foes alike that the family is alive and healthy. Good night and God bless you.

Dobson's participation in White House activities has continued with the Bush administration, although he has attempted in recent years to let Gary Bauer carry the larger responsibility. "As important as those governmental assignments are," he says today, "they are exhausting, and I assure you, they are thankless!"

Indeed, he is still attempting to cope with a thirty-million-dollar lawsuit brought against every member of the Pornography Commission by *Playboy* and *Penthouse* magazines. Unbelievably, these eleven citizens who gave fifteen months of their lives in the service of their country—traveling every month and reviewing the most wretched material on the face of the earth—are still, nearly four years later, under financial duress from this lawsuit. One of the most liberal judges in the Northeast, U.S. District Judge John Garrett Penn, has held a summary motion for dismissal on his desk for thirty-nine months, as of this writing. He simply will not rule one way or the other. This is the reward given to busy people who worked, without remuneration, on the Commission for countless hours and endured merciless criticism from the press and the pornographers. Perhaps *this* is why so many good and decent citizens choose not to get involved in government. Those on the liberal side *do* participate, however, because many of them earn a living by getting their share of grants, research dollars, and governmental influence.

Still, Dr. James Dobson can be heard month after month, calling for his countrymen to participate in the battle to save the family. He wrote a few weeks ago, "(at times) I feel like an army scout who has been sent forward to observe the position of the enemy. What I have seen has so alarmed me that I have been pleading for reinforcements ever since. A vast army is amassed on the next ridge in preparation for a strike. Doesn't anyone notice? Doesn't anyone care? Where are our troops? Why haven't they arrived? Don't the commanders know we haven't a minute to spare? Hello! Hello! Come in, America. Are you there?"

Again at the heart of Dobson's involvement in the political arena is his concern for the youngest and most vulnerable members of our society. Let me share the words he wrote in 1987 upon his return from an eight-week trip to London. Being there gave him an opportunity to observe the impact on future generations when a society forgets its spiritual heritage. These were his thoughts:

Traditional Judeo-Christian values literally hang in the balance [in America]. They can be "forgotten" in a single generation if they are not taught to children and teenagers. That loss of spiritual consciousness has already occurred in Great Britain, where 80 percent of the people attended church 40 years ago. I'm told the figure now is 4 percent! A generation of young people in Western Europe is also growing up today with *no* memory of the Christian faith, no awareness of its spiritual heritage. It could happen here if we don't defend what we believe.

Yet Congress continues to pour millions of dollars into organizations that despise our heritage, such as Planned Parenthood and the homosexual movement. It grants nothing to Focus on the Family (we wouldn't take it if it were offered) and very little to other conservative organizations like ours. Thus, with all the resources stacking on one side of the ledger, including the power of the press, our point of view is in serious jeopardy. Unless Christians care enough to defend their concept of morality, fidelity, and parental leadership, it will continue to erode. For my part, I've concluded that enough is enough. We will fight to protect today's children and teenagers from the ravages of hell, and we need the involvement of those who share our concern.

Dr. Dobson's longtime friend, Jim Davis, explained the passion that is so evident in these remarks. "I think there are a few things that really grieve Dobson's heart," Davis told me. "The most important is the moral decay of our nation and the destruction of our youth. The Bible asks, 'If the foundations be destroyed, what can the righteous do?' (Ps. 11:3). Jim Dobson sees a segment of our society that is putting the pursuit of pleasure above everything else and ignoring the disintegration of our young people. He sees the destruction of our value system, and that really disturbs him," Davis concluded. "It should grieve us all."

10

Champion for the Underdog

One of the most prominent traits of James Dobson's personality and professional career is his compassion for the underdog. His friends will tell you that he is a sucker for lost puppies, kids with big eyes, and everyone with a genuine need.

This identification with the down-and-out has become a characteristic of Focus on the Family as well. In recent years the ministry has directed its resources into helping the homeless, providing gifts for prison inmates, raising funds for a Mexican orphanage, and assisting refugee families in Central America. But even before such an organization existed, Dobson was devoted to helping the less fortunate and, even more to the point, assisting the powerless in coping with their oppression.

Jim Davis said it best, "Jim is a crusader, especially in the area of injustice. For example, he hates to see children treated unfairly, whether by their parents or even by a society that would expose them to pornography and filth. Those things really tug at his heart . . . probably because of his background at Children's Hospital."

This concern for the powerless and for people in need can be seen in the way Dobson functioned as a psychologist in the early days. Again, Jim Davis puts it in perspective, "In those years, the vast majority of his counseling was done for free. And that's because he really cared for people. I've always been amazed that no matter how busy he was, he would take time to listen and to pray with those in need."

One such incident occurred in 1969, shortly after he had been licensed as a psychologist in the state of California. The hour was after midnight when the telephone rang in the Dobsons' house. On the line was a troubled young man named David, whom Jim had been trying to help for several months. David's parents had severely rejected him, and he was lost, lonely, and confused. On this occasion, however, he was also drunk and suicidal.

"I am going to kill myself tonight," he said with slurred speech. "I have a gun here, and I'm going to use it unless you come to my house right now."

After talking to David at length, Dobson was convinced the young man meant business. He dressed, told Shirley he would be back in an hour or two, and drove out into the night. The address David had given him was located down a dark alley. After driving back and forth several times, Dobson spotted the correct street number on a little house in the shadows. He parked the car, got out, and knocked on the door.

A bleary-eyed nineteen year old appeared and asked him to come in. "Sit right there," he ordered, pointing to a chair. Dobson complied.

Then David walked on wobbly legs into the bathroom, which was in Dobson's line of vision. There, he reached behind the toilet and retrieved a .45 caliber pistol.

Suddenly, Dobson realized his precarious circumstances. There he was in the house of a drunk young man who cared little for his life. Maybe he had invited Dobson there to kill him. Who would ever find his body in that forsaken alley? he thought. Shirley had no idea where he had gone.

With the weapon in his hand and a gleam in his eye, David walked toward Dobson. The psychologist had only a few seconds to decide what to do. Should he spring at the teenager and attempt to wrestle the gun away—or just wait and hope? Neither answer seemed satisfactory.

David walked within three feet of his guest and stopped, giving Dobson one split second to lunge for the pistol. Just then, however, the young man turned the gun in his palm and offered it in a gesture of surrender. "I would have used this on myself tonight if you hadn't come," he said. Jim breathed a concealed sigh of relief and then began to counsel with the disturbed young man.

Although it has been many years since Dobson has made a midnight "house call," he is still sought after by those who want a word of counsel in the moment or two he can give them. Often we will dash out of the office in the middle of the day to grab a quick bite of lunch. Invariably, someone will recognize him and interrupt his meal to say "hello" or to seek his advice about some personal situation.

Dobson seems oblivious to the food on his plate, which gets colder by the moment. He listens to the person's situation with complete concentration and empathy. Never once have I heard him grumble afterwards about the delay or the ruined meal that resulted from the impromptu counseling session. In fact, Dobson seems to thrive on the opportunity to help.

His personal assistant, Dee Otte, confirms this compassionate characteristic. "He can be dead tired, but he will always stop to talk to people and pray with them. He simply has a genuine concern for others," she says.

Judy Berry, a close family friend, verifies this aspect of Jim's nature. "One thing you notice about him is that he is always looking for ways to reach out to people," she says. "At church, Jim stands and shakes hands and converses with people. He doesn't treat them according to class or money or who they are. He doesn't set himself apart. He mingles. He's gracious. After the morning service, it is difficult for the Dobsons to get away because Jim is just flooded by folks who want to meet him. I've seen people with books in their hands lined up after church just to get an autograph.

"I can also give you a personal example of how he reached out to me. One Sunday morning before church I came into the sanctuary looking for a place to sit. (My husband, Paul, was in the choir so I was by myself.) I saw Jim and Shirley down in front, and there was an available seat next to them. When I approached them, they greeted me warmly. Then Jim asked me how I was doing.

"I had really been struggling with a personal issue, and Jim could sense that. I just shook my head in response to his question. 'You're hurting, aren't you,' he said. He knew the issue that was bothering me, and he took out a notebook and he started writing. During the entire service, he wrote a magnificent analysis of the problem and proposed a solution. What he wrote that day set into motion the healing that has now become complete. But that's the kind of compassion he has. He had gone to sit and worship, but, instead, he sensed my pain and spent the entire service helping to lessen it."

The origin of this soft heart for others can probably be traced back to his father, who loved to give to those in need. Dr. Dobson explained this influence in his book *Straight Talk to Men and Their Wives:*

Of all the values transmitted to me by my father, none made a more lasting impression than his attitude toward money. As an evangelist, he could never depend on the compensation he would be given. The local church would collect a freewill offering for my father, but many times the gifts were barely sufficient to pay his traveling expenses. Furthermore, he would usually stay with the pastor during a ten-day revival; while there he often observed that the children needed shoes or books or medication. On the final night of the meeting when the modest offering was given to him, my dad would take enough money to get home and then donate the balance to meet the needs of the pastor's family.

Then my dad would return to be greeted by my mother and me. I can still hear the conversations between my good parents.

"Did you have a successful revival?" my mother would ask.

"The Lord was with us," my dad would reply.

"How much did they pay you?"

"Well, I need to talk to you about that," my father would say, grinning.

"I know," Mom would say. "You gave it all away, didn't you?"

My mother would invariably sanction his decision, saying if my dad felt that way it was all right. God had always taken good care of us and would continue to do so.

A few days later when the bills began to accumulate, our little family would gather on our knees before the Lord. Dad would pray first.

"Lord, you know we've been faithful with the resources you've given us. We've tried to be responsive to the needs of others when you laid them on our hearts. Now, Lord, *my* family is in need. You've said, *'Give and it shall be given unto you.'* So we bring to you our empty meal barrel and ask you to fill it."

As a child, I listened intently to these prayers and watched carefully to see how God responded. I tell you without exaggeration that money invariably arrived in the next few days. God did not make us rich, as some ministers promise today. But He never let us go hungry. On one occasion, $1200 arrived in the mail the day after this hard up family prayer. My childlike faith grew by leaps and bounds at this demonstration of trust and sacrifice by my father and mother. I regret that my own children have never seen their parents forced to depend on God in the way I experienced as a boy.

One year, Jim's father went to the bank a few days before Christmas and exchanged a twenty-dollar bill for twenty, crisp, new, one-dollar bills. Then he attached a Merry Christmas note to the bills and gave them to people in the neighborhood. He gave one each to the newsboy, the shoeshine man, the mailman, and others. It was his way of saying he cared for them.

Whether or not young Jim inherited his sensitivity to people or simply learned it from his parents is unclear. It *is* known that this characteristic surfaced early in his life. His mother affirmed that he had a very tender heart even as a preschooler. One day the family drove past a ragged, dirty little boy walking along the road, and five-year-old Jimmy began to cry. He wanted to go back and offer to help the poor lad.

An Italian boy lived in the neighborhood where young Jim grew up. Other children rejected him and called him a "Dago." America was fighting World War II at the time, and children of German, Japanese, and Italian descent were often mocked and teased. Although Jim was only five years old, he felt that the Italian boy was not being treated fairly. He promptly left the company of the "in" group and chose to play with his harassed friend.

His genuine care for those in need and those who suffer explains why Dr. Dobson wrote the following statement as one of the four foundational principles upon which Focus on the Family is based:

We believe that human life is of inestimable worth and significance in all its dimensions, including the aged, the widowed, the mentally retarded, the unattractive, the physically handicapped, the various races, and every other condition in which humanness is expressed from conception to the grave, including the unborn.

For this reason Dr. Dobson has been a vocal champion of the unborn. Who could be more vulnerable, more defenseless than the tiny baby who resides in his mother's womb? He can be torn to pieces or poisoned in a salt solution with complete impunity under the law. He is unable to plead his own case and is not even anesthetized while being dismembered. He has no rights. Rarely in human history has a class of human beings faced such merciless discrimination and brutality. However, there was one other period of violence that comes to mind, and Dobson wrote about it in 1988. He was asked by the editors of *Life* magazine to comment on the subject of abortion. This was his response:

After World War II, German citizens living around Nazi extermination camps were required to visit the facilities to witness the atrocities they had permitted to occur. Though it was technically "legal" to kill Jews and other political prisoners, the citizens were blamed for not breaking the law in deference to a higher moral code. This is the way we feel about the slaughter of 25 million unborn children. Some of them are being burned to death by a salt solution only days before a normal delivery would have occurred. This is a moral outrage that transcends the law which sanitizes the killings. We are law-abiding people and do not advocate violence or obscene and disrespectful behavior, but to be sure, we will follow that higher moral code nonviolently, to rescue innocent, defenseless babies. And someday, the moral issues involved here will be as clear to the world as the Nazi holocaust is today.

The unborn child is the ultimate underdog!

In a sense, the institution of the family also shares underdog status. It is beleaguered by divorce, alcoholism, drug abuse, financial problems, infidelity, and problems too numerous to mention. For the past two decades, Dr. Dobson has worked tirelessly to defend the traditional family from those who attack it because they believe it has outlived its usefulness.

A clear picture of that threat emerged in July 1989 as the New York Court of Appeals expanded its definition of the family to include gay lovers, thereby granting them certain benefits formerly reserved for spouses. Several city councils across the United States also acknowledged the legality of homosexual relationships by awarding bereavement benefits, sick leaves, and hospital visitation rights to city employees with "domestic partners." The National Gay and Lesbian Task Force anticipates the day when homosexual relationships will be granted full marital status by the courts.

For these reasons and many more James Dobson has worked tirelessly on behalf of the family. He has been called "America's Family Advocate"—a title that suits him well.

Another underdog that has captured Dr. Dobson's attention was mentioned at the same banquet where President Reagan had spoken. Grace Nelson, wife of Congressman Bill Nelson from Florida, made this simple statement that so accurately summarized the psychologist's life mission: "When I think of Dr. Dobson, I think of the children."

Mrs. Nelson was absolutely correct in this assessment, echoing the observation by Jim Davis, who was mentioned earlier. No other subject more strongly inspires Dobson's passions for protection and defense. Today's young are among the most vulnerable underdogs in our society, and his heart breaks for them.

If James Dobson's epitaph could be contained in only one sentence, it would undoubtedly state that he was a champion for the children. It has been that way since his early career as a teacher and counselor. During his graduate program he studied child development, and at Children's Hospital he devoted his time to researching new ways to prevent mental retardation.

He became a public defender of children in the 1970s by writing several books about their needs. I pressed him once to tell me which of his books was his favorite. *"Hide or Seek,"* he responded, "because it best describes what makes children tick."

Another early book, *Preparing for Adolescence,* was addressed directly to boys and girls on the eve of their teen experience. Four hundred thousand children have now read the book or have heard the audio tapes. In response, many of these kids write to tell Dr. Dobson their problems because they know they can trust him. The following letter is typical of the "pain mail" that flows into Focus on the Family every day:

Dear Dr. Dobson,

I am fifteen and very lonely and depressed. I feel so awkward and inadequate in front of my peers. I have entered into a self-help group with our school psychologist and one of our counselors. The only problem is that I'm too intimidated to speak. I wish I could feel better, but it's so hard. To make things worse, I have an older sister. She is the perfect one. She has all the friends, good grades, beauty, and one of the best things—self-esteem! Once, when she wanted to be a cheerleader, I talked Mom out of it because I was so jealous.

My sister is lean. I'm not. It hurts when I stand next to a thin person who complains about her own weight. If she thinks she is fat, what does she think about me?

I've been called many names. In the fourth grade I was called Moose. Next came Guinea Pig. Now, I'm a fat Magic Marker and everyone else is a skinny pencil. Since I am this way, people tend to stay away from me, and my friends are considered losers.

I don't know which way to turn. I have to resolve this conflict. I've contemplated suicide, but what good will that do? I won't be around to feel better. Besides, I'm chicken. I just don't know what to do!

What deep pain and loneliness this young girl feels! And yet, she speaks for large numbers within a generation who are growing up in a world so very different from the one their parents knew twenty or thirty years ago.

Today's teenager is exposed to such evil influences as dial-a-porn, slasher films, and satanic lyrics in rock music. These sinister forces have been marketed to our young by greedy entrepreneurs who have no regard for the lasting impact of their messages.

When you consider these influences in addition to the explicit and amoral sex education programs being provided in many schools, one has to wonder how any of our kids develop respect for Judeo-Christian values.

James Dobson's greatest irritation and regret is the kind of environment our society has created for our children. He conveyed this concern in a letter to his constituents in 1987. I believe it is one of the most moving and visionary statements he has ever written.

I recently saw a fascinating television documentary on the subject of elephants and their behavioral characteristics. The program was videotaped in India, where the magnificent pachyderms are trained to serve their human masters. Of course, if elephants knew how strong they were, they would never yield to the domination of anything, but they are subjected to a stressful form of "brainwashing," which takes the fight out of them. The process begins with three days of total isolation from man or beast. Female elephants and their young are remarkably social animals. They grieve and fret and long for their peers. At that precise moment of vulnerability, they are brought to a nighttime ceremony of fire. Then for many hours in the flickering light, they are screamed at, intimidated, stroked and ordered back and forth. By morning, half-crazed, the elephants have yielded. Their wills have been broken. Man is the master.

Even though I understand the economic need for working elephants in India, there is still something sad about their plight. These wonderfully intelligent animals are transformed from freedom to slavery in a single evening. Their fragile emotions are manipulated to destroy their independence and curb their individuality. Somehow, I wish it weren't true.

Then as I watched the documentary, I was struck by the parallel between these elephants and us fragile human beings. We too are social creatures, born with irrepressible needs to be loved and accepted by our parents and peers. In fact, to deprive us of this emotional support during early childhood is to risk crippling us for life.

But if our needs for love are great during childhood, they can't compare with the soul hunger we feel with the arrival of adolescence. Like the elephants staked in a distant field, teenagers are subjected by their culture to a period of intense isolation and loneliness. Even those who are moderately successful during these years often feel rejected, ridiculed, and ignored. Unfortunately for the most tender and pliable among us, the pain of adolescence can be incalculable. These youngsters slink through the halls of their schools, looking at the floor and fearing the wrath of their peers. They are, at that moment, prime targets for brainwashing.

Adolescent society will do the rest. Anyone who has worked with teenagers has surely witnessed this mind-bending process at work. Television and movies hammer away at moral values and principles. Friends and acquaintances ridicule any form of self-discipline or restraint.

But the analogy to the conditioning of elephants becomes even more striking. Rock concerts subject masses of needy kids to deafening noises, strange lights, wild emotions, and godless philosophies. Like an elephant during the night of fire, an adolescent begins to lose his grip on reality. His fight to preserve individuality slowly ebbs away. A passion for conformity rises from deep within. His peer group becomes lord and master, until finally, the wonderful freedom of youth is traded for slavery and peer dependency.

This conditioning process helps explain the irrationality of youth. Why else would healthy boys and girls inject wretched drugs into their veins—or give sexual favors to a virtual stranger—or dye their hair orange and green—or even commit suicide? Their behavior has been warped by enormous social pressures in an environment of unmet needs. Now obviously, teenagers possess a free will, and I would not excuse those who engage in irresponsible behavior. But they are also victims—victims of a peer-dominated society that can only leave them lost and confused. And my heart goes out to them.

How passionately I feel about the plight of today's children. How sorry I am for the pressures we have allowed to engulf them. How regretful I am for the sexual enticements that reach their ears during elementary school, teaching them that virginity is a curse and sex is an adolescent toy. How I grieve for the boys and girls who have been told, and now they believe, that they are utter fools and will fail in each of life's endeavors. How tender I feel toward the wounded children, the blind or deaf or retarded or cerebral palsied, who believe themselves to be cursed by God and man. Somehow, we must make a new effort to reach this generation with a message of confidence and hope and love and respect. And ultimately, we must secure the gospel of Jesus Christ in their hearts and protect it from the assault of hell.

That is my profound desire at this stage of my life. The Lord has laid a new burden on me in recent weeks—urging me to feed not only His *sheep*, but also His *lambs*.

In the years since he wrote this letter, Dr. Dobson has increased his emphasis on ministry to the young. Focus on the Family has launched four monthly youth magazines, a weekly radio program for kids, and a series of dramatic videos designed to teach spiritual values to children. But these are only props and tools for imparting scriptural themes. The real work of rescuing the next generation from the evil forces in society belongs to the parents.

To this end, Dobson has called upon parents to protect the morality of their children and to resist the forces that would tear marriages apart. All too often Dobson has seen the devastating effects of divorce upon the little ones. In conclusion, allow me to share a poem he received from one young lady whose parents had divorced. The grief she expresses in these verses is all one needs to understand why Dr. Dobson is a champion for the children.

Does a Child Understand?

Such a touchy topic—
Does a child understand?
The gradual separation
Of a woman and a man?
Flashbacks haunt my thoughts—
Those scary, scary words.
Why can't I just erase
The threats I overheard?

Mommy's body pushed,
The vase that's on the floor,
Mommy crying, in such pain,
Dad runs out the door.
I'm frozen in the recurrent scene—
No crying nor speaking—WHY?
I'm filled with fear and sorrow
But no tear slips from my eye.

"Don't tell anyone," I am told.
Yes, all right, I won't.
But what if . . . ? "No! Not anyone!"
Oh. Then, of course, I don't.
Gone is the caring—
The family I want to be.
In its place there's something horrid—
Lying, pretending, enmity.

Does a child understand
The sudden coldness in the air,
The rotten words that fly about,
The nights when one's not there?
The crescendo of the hatred builds—
I cover my ears with my hands.
Why them, why me, why *my* family?
I do not understand.

                              Stephanie Fan

11

A Final Look

One of the most fascinating aspects of my close association with Dr. James Dobson has been the opportunity to observe the remarkable pace at which his ministry has grown. In just twelve years the size of his daily radio audience has expanded beyond 3 million, according to some analysts. More than 2 million households receive his monthly magazine. His films have been viewed by approximately 100 million people. There appears to be no end in sight to this phenomenal growth. Approximately 30,000 new people add their names to the Focus on the Family mailing list every month.

The impact he has had on evangelicals in North America is unprecedented. In March 1988 the World Home Bible League announced results of a survey that supported this idea. From a list of 8,500 organizations, respondents selected Focus on the Family as their "most favored" ministry, and Dobson was the most respected Christian leader.

But neither statistics nor polls can adequately explain the influence James Dobson is having on so many people. It is best understood when we have the privilege of meeting the individuals whose lives are represented by these numbers. How often I have been warmly welcomed into someone's home because I represent this ministry. Immediately, I notice that their shelves are lined with books offered by Focus on the Family and their coffee table is covered with the ministry's periodicals. Invariably, my hosts begin to share how some extension of Dr. Dobson's outreach contributed to their family's welfare. With tears of appreciation welling up in their eyes they say:

"Our marriage was pulled back from the brink of disaster."

"I regained control of my finances."

"I connected with my teenage son for the first time in years."

"I discovered that my child has a learning disorder."

"I decided to keep my baby instead of getting an abortion."

After so many of these emotional encounters, I am struck not only by the breadth of Dr. Dobson's influence but by its depth as well. Everywhere I turn I meet people whose lives *have been changed*!

Recently I was speaking at a writers' conference, and when I invited questions from the floor, one woman stood up and said, "I don't want to ask a question. I would like to make a statement. I would just like to comment on my love and respect for Dr. Dobson." She continued with her remarks and explained how the psychologist had helped her.

As a member of Focus on the Family's leadership team, I am often asked by curious friends to explain the phenomenon behind James Dobson. "What is the secret of his success?" they want to know. "Why does he have such a powerful impact on people?"

Although these are straightforward questions, there really is no simple answer. These questions were in the forefront of my mind when I undertook to write this book. I hoped to find an adequate response that would explain Dobson's success by exploring the principles by which he lives. In so doing, my desire was to help others live more fruitful lives.

Now, after eight years of interviews, observations, and meetings with Dr. Dobson and those who know him well, I have concluded that the answer is twofold.

First, I believe that he has been uniquely blessed by God. I heard this comment from scores of his colleagues, but it is apparent even to the casual observer. Why has the Lord placed His hand on James Dobson in such a special way? I can't begin to understand the mind of God and why He chooses to touch some individuals and not others. But I have no doubt that God's blessing is, in part, a response to the thousands of prayers uttered by George McCluskey, Jim's great-grandfather, four generations ago and then by his grandparents and finally his mother and father. The Lord has obviously reached across time and honored those petitions from the past.

Noble Hathaway, a close and longtime friend of the Dobson family, agrees. "The prayer life of Jim's forebears is the answer to why his ministry has been so blessed," he told me. "Many years ago, my wife and I used to vacation with Myrtle and Jim, Sr. I remember vividly how they used to sit up late at night during our travels and pray for their little boy. They really had a burden for his spiritual condition, and they desperately wanted to be united in heaven. I think it's safe to say that Dr. Dobson has had more prayers uttered on his behalf than anyone I know. Now I'm seventy-one years old, retired and on the shelf. Jim, Sr., Myrtle, and my wife, Gwendolyn, have all gone to be with the Lord. For some reason, God has allowed me to remain here. So, I have committed my remaining days to continue the ministry of prayer that Dr. Dobson's parents started. Every morning before breakfast, I have a one-man prayer meeting for Jim, Shirley, Danae, and Ryan. I am committed to bombarding the skies with prayers for the Dobsons."

No doubt many people today share a similar burden for Dr. Dobson and his family. Their petitions for God's blessings offer the best explanation I can find for Dr. Dobson's fruitfulness.

In the same way, I believe that James Dobson's ministry has been the fulfillment of his father's vision for reaching multitudes with the gospel message. To some extent, Dr. Dobson is the inheritor of a tremendous spiritual legacy and mantle.

Second, I have concluded that James Dobson's ministry has flourished because of his own commitment to godly living. There is another term to describe this lifestyle, but I am reluctant to use it because it sounds terribly old-fashioned and may even carry theological overtones. Nevertheless, it answers the questions very succinctly: Jim Dobson has reaped a harvest because of his dedication to *holiness*.

Family friend Judy Berry offers another valuable perspective: "I don't think Jim ever set out to develop something that now exists as Focus on the Family. I think he first sought the kingdom of God. His first desire and goal in life was to walk in obedience to God. I believe Jim has been given a set of gifts by God that, because of his determination to walk in obedience, were allowed to blossom. It's also been a matter of right choices. Jim said to himself, 'I'm going to follow God because I believe in what He says and I believe in His character. I believe in my heritage. I've seen it in my mother and father. I've seen it in my family. I want it for myself. Regardless of what the consequences are, I believe in what God says, and if I seek Him first, all these other things will be added unto me.'"

Once again, let me offer the disclaimer that Dr. Dobson is not without his shortcomings. Some readers may be disappointed that I didn't focus more on his faults and flaws. That could have been done, although I could find no significant "skeletons" in the Dobsons' closet to be dragged into the light of day. As Judy Berry said, "What you see is what you get with Jim." On the other hand, even the most righteous and noble among us can be discredited and ridiculed if we focus the microscope exclusively on our blemishes. None of us can withstand that scrutiny. After all, we wouldn't need a savior if we enjoyed such perfection in the natural state. And James Dobson has inherited the same flawed, sinful nature as the rest of humanity.

My intent, however, has been to convey the positive, uplifting character of James Dobson without veering from the truth. The Apostle Paul instructed us to take this approach to life when he wrote, "whatever is true, whatever is noble, whatever is right, whatever is pure, whatever is lovely, whatever is admirable—if anything is excellent or praiseworthy—think about such things" (Phil. 4:8 NIV).

How different in perspective is the thrust of modern journalism. A reporter is considered almost unprofessional unless he portrays his subjects in a negative light. In Dobson's case, journalists for *Playboy* magazine, *The Wall Street Journal* and a major

Christian magazine have called his friends and said something like, "I've already heard the good, impressive things about James Dobson. Give me the other side. Tell me where his hidden problems are." It's a sign of the times.

Biographers today sell more books by revealing the wretched side of the people they describe. Likewise, the entire White House press corps seems to have only one overriding objective— to uncover something embarrassing, controversial, or illegal about the president. If they can find such a story, it will appear the next morning with a byline on page one. Good news, however, will be ignored or buried in Section E. In this world of anti-heroes and fallen leaders, it has been a pleasure to write about a man who simply is who he holds himself out to be, nothing more, nothing less. And my purpose has been not to aggrandize him or create a storybook fantasy, but to describe the godly principles that have guided his life. It is my hope that others will be motivated to adopt and apply them in their own lives.

These principles, which have been illustrated in the preceding pages, could be summed up as follows:

1. He has a keen sensitivity to God's presence.

Dobson believes that God is near him at all times, and he lives his life accordingly. As a result, the Lord has drawn close to him. In my mind, that helps to explain why God speaks to Jim in an almost audible way on various occasions. I think it also tells why Jim has never experienced a moral collapse. He knows that God is watching him, and he tries harder than most men to avoid blatant, willful sin.

2. He has a tremendous desire to learn.

Ever since his childhood, Dobson has been an eager disciple. He has been willing to learn from his parents, his teachers, his peers, and his subordinates. He approaches every day with wide-eyed curiosity and a sincere intent to expand his knowledge.

That love for life was apparent to me one afternoon when we were out for an afternoon drive. During the course of a single conversation, Jim talked about the development of nuclear fusion and the possibility that it might fulfill biblical prophecy ("the desert shall rejoice, and blossom as the rose," Isa. 35:1); the concept that there is no chronological time in heaven and what that might mean; and how the fundamental laws of physics apply to human relationships. Dobson's desire to learn emanates from an intense appreciation for the wonderful world God has created for us.

3. He has an appetite for hard work.

Dr. Dobson has the highest energy level of any person I have ever known. Men who are thirty years younger than he cannot keep up with his pace. He is a hard-driving, highly organized leader. In addition to writing books and creating a daily broadcast, he is an active chief executive officer of the Focus on the Family ministry. He takes his paperwork home in boxes (no briefcase is big enough) and labors over the "stack" until he is done. His colleagues are accustomed to late night phone calls from him that begin, "I was just reading your memo and . . ." This could be considered his greatest asset and his most glaring weakness. Fortunately, his penchant for work is balanced by his recreation on the basketball court, by his relationship with Shirley whom he loves to be with, and by his commitment to a day of rest and worship.

4. He has a commitment to excellence.

If you do it unto the Lord, he reasons, then you should do it well. As a result, almost everything Focus on the Family produces is done according to high standards. People who fail to achieve this level of performance often hear one of these gentle rebukes: "I'm sorry. That just doesn't get it done," or, "You didn't pay the price to do it right."

5. He is concerned with meeting the needs of others.

Whether he is preparing a speech for thousands or counseling a single troubled soul, Dobson's first priority is to meet needs. Many professional communicators or ministers miss the mark by dictating *their own* priorities to their audience. Dr. Dobson finds out what the *person's* needs are, and then comes alongside to assist.

172

6. He has a genuine respect for others.

This principle serves as a foundation for all his relationships. From this basis, he has formed many of his theories on marriage and parenting: husbands and wives should respect each other; children should obey their parents; likewise, workers should yield to those placed in authority over them; employers should treat their workers respectfully, etc. This word *respect* can be found throughout Dobson's books.

7. He believes in marital fidelity.

Many people have criticized Dr. Dobson for saying he would never be unfaithful to his wife. "Don't tempt the devil," they say. "Pride goeth before the fall." But these well-meaning critics don't understand the depth of Jim's conviction about adultery, which he views as the ultimate breach of respect in a relationship. Once, as our executive team was meeting, someone walked into the room with news that another Christian leader had been discovered in an extramarital affair. After praying about the situation, Dr. Dobson looked around the table and asked, "Is anyone living the life? Who can we trust?" Although he knows that God will forgive even the sin of adultery, he views fidelity as a cornerstone in his relationship with Shirley and with God.

8. He is generous.

Dr. Dobson learned at an early age that you cannot outgive God. I vividly remember standing one night on the porch of one of the beautiful mansions built by the late tycoon Charles Wrigley. "Isn't this estate incredible?" I exclaimed. "I'm not impressed," Jim responded. "Wrigley poured his fortune into building this place, and in a few years it will be reduced to rubble. I would rather put my money into things that have eternal value." Those words have been validated in my observation of James Dobson, who still lives in the house he and Shirley purchased seventeen years ago. He is simply the most generous person I have known.

9. He believes in accountability.

Dobson believes that people perform better and are more righteous when they are accountable to one another. Thus, he maintains that every person, including himself, should report to someone. Through the years Dr. Dobson has willingly submitted himself to his independent Board of Directors. He seeks their supervision and the security it provides. By the same token, he can be demanding of those who work for him. He expects results. His adherence to this management philosophy is built upon his knowledge that one day God will hold each of us accountable for our actions.

10. He has integrity.

Nothing means more to James Dobson than his reputation for integrity. Tim Stafford, writing in *Christianity Today*, once commented, "Friends and coworkers, when asked to describe Dobson, tend to revert to one word—integrity. They mean, among other things, that he is the same at home as he is on the stage." Bob Screen, a consultant to the ministry, applies that word to the way Dobson raises money from his supporters. "James Dobson wouldn't want a nickel from someone who was struggling financially," Screen says. "He simply has always had a higher priority. He has never been willing to compromise spiritual priorities, personal integrity, or a sense of appropriateness in order to advance his organization. He cares more about his constituents than building his ministry."

11. He believes we must fight to preserve our values.

His efforts in the public policy arena come from a sincere conviction that Christians have a responsibility to mold and shape their society. In his film "A Winnable War," Dr. Dobson described a revelation he experienced one afternoon at a meeting of the Attorney General's Commission on Pornography. This event became a significant impetus in his efforts to enlist people in the battle to save the family.

At breaktime, I left the other commissioners and went to the window to look down on the city below. We were on the twenty-eighth floor of a skyscraper in downtown Chicago. I noticed a building immediately across from me that was being demolished. A crane was swinging a huge wrecking ball into the structure, sending debris and dust in all directions. As I watched, the thought suddenly struck me:

"That's what they're doing to my country. Those who hate the institution of the family are hammering away at it with a wrecking ball. They are undermining its foundation and shattering its support systems. Don't they know that the family is necessary to the stability of the edifice? If they are successful in destroying it, the entire superstructure of society will come crashing down with it!"

That's when I resolved to do my best on that commission. I committed myself to mobilize as many Americans and Canadians as possible to *get involved* in the battle to protect our families.

12. He has surrounded himself with quality people.

From the earliest days of the ministry, when his friend Gil Moegerle joined him in the studio, Dobson has looked for the most qualified people to help him carry the load. Through the ensuing years, an incredible team has been assembled at the Pomona headquarters. In fact, Tony Wauterlek, a member of the Board of Directors and a man with broad business experience, recently commented that he has never seen a harder working or more dedicated staff than the Focus team. Others agree. It is led by a group of vice-presidents, each of whom is a specialist in a particular field. From the switchboard operator, to the hundreds of people who work in broadcasting, public affairs, cassette duplication, listener services, accounting, correspondence, counseling, publications, film production, book publishing, shipping, or the tour guide department, God has truly blessed the ministry with a "family" of dedicated workers. Dobson acknowledges today that the Focus ministry is no one-man band. It is truly a team effort.

13. He believes in maintaining a committed prayer life.

Dr. Dobson has never made a major move in his life without submitting the matter to prayer. But he also converses regularly with God about the little things as well. He is always talking with his Lord. Whether he is driving alone in the car, taking a walk around the block with Shirley, or bidding farewell to guests, he uses these occasions to communicate with God. Pastor Donald Bowen of Alexandria, Virginia, wrote the following column in his church bulletin after a chance encounter with Dr. Dobson more than 2,500 miles from Dobson's home.

As I stood in line at Popeye's restaurant, I could not help but notice the man behind me. He looked so familiar. Since I wasn't quite sure, I did not say anything at the time. Being ahead of him, I got my order, sat down and began to eat. In just a few minutes he did the same. All the time I was eating, I kept saying to myself, "I know that man." Determined to find out who he was before he or I left, I approached him on the way out and asked, "Excuse me, sir, but do you live in Alexandria?" Pleasantly, he told me he did not. I asked, "Do you live in California?" When he said he did, I responded, "You are Dr. James Dobson, aren't you?" He acknowledged that he was.

What a delightful surprise! I had gone to Popeye's for a piece of chicken and met the best-known author, lecturer, and spokesman on the family in America today! We chatted for a few minutes about our church, my family, and his ministry. He asked that I extend to you a personal word from him since we have shared his films and have his books in our church library.

That's the story as it happened last week, but I haven't told you everything. As I sat there in Popeye's, I felt sure the man a few tables away was Dr. Dobson. But what would *he* be doing in Popeye's? The thing that clinched it in my own thinking was a small thing he did before eating. He simply bowed his head and silently gave thanks for his food. He, of course, did not know that I was watching, but when I saw him do it, I thought to myself, "That has to be Dr. James Dobson."

I share the story because he asked me to bring you greetings. But there is another reason—to remind you that a simple act, such as a silent blessing in a restaurant, can be a witness to somebody. We just never know, do we, who might be watching? Dr. Dobson didn't know that I was!

Finally, there is one more principle that guides the behavior of James Dobson.

14. He has a strong awareness of the brevity of life.

Of all the principles he learned from his father, this one has had the greatest impact on him. He often says that our time on earth is a very brief experience and it requires discipline to get through the tough moments and temptations that come our way. "We must live every day as though it were our last," he says, "because this short life will soon be over, and we will be standing before our Lord."

A few years ago, Jim and I were driving home from a mountain climbing trip in the Sierra Nevada range where we had enjoyed the fellowship of several other fathers and their children. Spending three days away from the routine of city life had given us an opportunity to reflect on the most important priorities in our lives. The five-hour drive home gave us ample time to share our feelings about many of the principles important to us. Then we talked about the brevity of life, and Dr. Dobson made this comment. "You know, Rolf," he said, "I would feel satisfied if I could achieve just three goals with my life."

"What are they?" I asked.

"First, I want to stand before my Creator and hear the words: 'Well done thou good and faithful servant. Enter into the joy of the Lord.'

"Second, I want to take as many people as possible to heaven with me.

"Third, I want to be reunited with my family in heaven. I want to see my parents again. I want Shirley to be there, and I want to spend eternity with my children."

A few years later, I had an opportunity to hear Jim speak about this third goal and how it related to the brevity of life. He was addressing a small group of very special friends who had gathered to dedicate the Hugo W. Schoellkopf, III Memorial Conference Center at Focus on the Family's headquarters. This event was held in honor of Hugo Schoellkopf, a former member of Focus' Board, who had died in a plane crash along with three other friends of the ministry: Creath Davis, George Clark, and Dr. Trevor Maybery. To that gathering of friends, Dr. Dobson spoke the following words, which serve as a proper conclusion to this book. May these thoughts about living with eternity's values in view help you to find significance in the principles of godly living I have tried to capture on these pages.

Some of you know that I was with Pete Maravich when he died two weeks ago. He had come to California to be a guest on our radio program, and I invited him to play basketball with us the morning before our scheduled interview. It was an audacious thing to do. Pete was one of the greatest basketball players to ever walk on a court, and he still holds many records at LSU and in the National Basketball Association. Nevertheless, he agreed to play a "pick up" game with us at 7 A.M.

Pete had not been feeling well for nearly a year, complaining about neuralgia in his right shoulder. So, he didn't "hustle" that morning, and there were only brief flashes of his former greatness. We played for about forty-five minutes and then the guys took a brief break. As Pete and I stood on the court, I asked him, "How can you just give up this great game? It's meant too much to you through the years."

"You know," he replied, "I agree with you. I think I'll start playing again in casual competition like this. But I haven't been able to do anything for almost a year. Up until a week ago, I couldn't lift a two-pound ball over my head because of my shoulder."

"How are you feeling today?" I asked.

"I just feel great" was his answer.

Those were his last words on this earth. Pete turned to walk away, and as he did, he suddenly fell to the floor. He did not attempt to break his fall with his hands. He hit the court hard.

I walked to his side, thinking he was kidding. For one of the world's great athletes to say, "I feel great," and then fall was the kind of joke for which Pete was known. But when I looked in his eyes, I saw that he was having a seizure. I cradled his head and attempted to keep his air passage open. That lasted for about twenty seconds, and then . . . Pete died in my arms. He never took another breath.

I screamed for the other players to come help me, and within a few seconds we were giving him CPR. But his heart never beat again. He was gone. The autopsy revealed later that Pete had a congenital malformation of the heart. Whereas most of us have two coronary arterial systems that wrap around the heart, Pete only had one. He was destined to drop dead from the moment of his birth, and only God knows why it happened during that brief encounter when his path crossed mine.

The shock of Pete's untimely death is impossible to describe. None of the men who witnessed the tragedy will ever forget it. I am just grateful that he knew the Lord and had been so diligent in spreading the good news about Jesus Christ. Pete was ready to meet his Maker, there's no doubt about that. But my heart goes out to his lovely wife Jackie and their two sons, Jaeson and Joshua. I spoke at his funeral three days later and feel a bond of kinship with his little family.

When I came home from the gymnasium on the afternoon following Pete's death, I sat down with Ryan and discussed the circumstance. (He was seventeen years old at the time.) Then I said to him, "Ryan, I want you to understand what has happened here. Pete's death was not an unusual tragedy that has happened to only one man and his family. We all must face death sooner or later and in one way or the other. This is the 'human condition' of which I have spoken. For some people, it comes too early, and for others too late. But no one will escape, ultimately. And, of course, it will also happen to me. So, without being morbid about it, I want you to begin to prepare yourself for that time. Sooner or later, you'll get the kind of phone call that Mrs. Maravich received today. It could occur ten or fifteen years from now, but it will come eventually. And when it does happen, there is *one* thought I want to leave with you. I don't know if I'll have an opportunity to give you my 'last words' then, so let me express them to you right now. Freeze frame this moment in your mind, and hold onto it for the rest of your life. My message to you is *Be There!* Be there to meet your mother and me in heaven. We will be looking for you on that glad morning. Don't let anything deter you from keeping that appointment. Because I am fifty-one years old and you are only seventeen, as many as fifty years could pass from the time of my death to yours. That's a long time to remember. But you can be sure that I will be searching for you just inside the Eastern Gate. This is the only thing of real significance in your life. I care what you accomplish in the years to come, and I hope you make good use of the great potential the Lord has given to you. But above every other purpose and goal, the only thing that really matters is that you determine now to *Be There!*"

That message to Ryan is not only the most important thought I could express to my son. It is also the heart and soul of what I have tried to convey to this present generation. *Be There!* That must be our ultimate objective in living! I believe our four friends who died in the plane crash last year would confirm that goal for their wives and children, if they could speak to them tonight. It is what Fook Kong Li would say if he were with us this evening. I know, also, that it is what my father would express as the central theme of his life.

Finally, that is also what the ministry of Focus on the Family is all about. Yes, we say that our purpose is to preserve families and make married life more meaningful. That is true. But it is a secondary objective. Our *primary* reason for existence is to cooperate with the Holy Spirit in the salvation of every person we can possibly reach. Preserving families, you see, is our way of accomplishing that goal. It is certainly the best avenue to reach the generation of children now coming on the scene. That is why we are here. That is why these facilities that we are dedicating tonight have been constructed. They do not represent a monument to Shirley or me. *Who cares* about such vainglory? In a few short years, we will be gone, and these beautiful buildings will belong to another organization. In the meantime, this is merely a convenient place to urge our friends . . . to *Be There*. Help us spread the word, won't you?

And so we conclude this book right where we began it—with a message from Dr. Dobson about the brevity of life and an exhortation to live with eternity's values in view. The Christian life is a terrific adventure. It is my ultimate hope that by reading about Dr. Dobson and his principles you have been encouraged to complete that journey and experience God's richest blessings along the way.

Biographical Information

James C. Dobson, Ph.D., is founder and president of Focus on the Family, a nonprofit organization that produces his nationally syndicated radio program, heard daily on more than 1300 stations.

He was for fourteen years an Associate Clinical Professor of Pediatrics at the University of Southern California School of Medicine and served for seventeen years on the Attending Staff of Children's Hospital of Los Angeles in the Division of Child Development and Medical Genetics. He has an earned Ph.D. from the University of Southern California in the field of child development, an Honorary Doctorate of Laws from Pepperdine University, an Honorary Doctorate of Humanities from Franciscan University of Steubenville, an Honorary Doctorate of Humane Letters from Seattle Pacific University, and an Honorary Doctorate of Humanities from Asbury Theological Seminary. He was honored in 1987 as "The Children's Friend" by CHILDHELP, an organization devoted to the prevention of child abuse. He received the Alumni Merit Award, 1989, from the University of Southern California General Alumni Association. He was also honored by the California State Psychological Association in recognition of Distinguished Humanitarian Contributions, 1988.

His first book for parents and teachers, *Dare to Discipline*, has now sold over one million copies and was selected as one of the fifty books to be rebound and placed in the White House

Library. His subsequent ten books for the family are also best sellers: *Hide or Seek, What Wives Wish Their Husbands Knew About Women, The Strong-Willed Child, Preparing for Adolescence, Straight Talk to Men and Their Wives, Emotions: Can You Trust Them?, Dr. Dobson Answers Your Questions, Love Must Be Tough, Love for a Lifetime,* and *Parenting Isn't For Cowards.*

His first film series, *Focus on the Family,* has now been seen by over sixty million people. His newest film series, *Turn Your Heart Toward Home,* was released in January 1986 and has been seen by thirty million viewers to date.

Dr. Dobson has been heavily involved in governmental activities related to the family. He served on the task force which summarized the White House Conferences on the Family and received a special commendation from President Jimmy Carter in 1980. He was appointed by President Ronald Reagan to the National Advisory Committee to the Office of Juvenile Justice and Delinquency Prevention, 1982–84. From 1984–87, he was regularly invited to the White House to consult with President Reagan and his staff on family matters. He served as cochairman of the Citizens Advisory Panel for Tax Reform, in consultation with President Reagan, and served as chairman of the United States Army Task Force Staff, 1986–88.

He was appointed to Attorney General Edwin Meese's Commission on Pornography, 1985–86. Dr. Dobson was also appointed in the spring of 1987 to the Attorney General's Advisory Board on Missing and Exploited Children and to Secretary Otis Bowen's Panel on Teen Pregnancy Prevention, within the Department of Health and Human Services. In October 1987, he received the Marian Pfister Anschutz Award in recognition of his contribution to the American family. A videotaped message of congratulations was sent by President Reagan. More recently, he was asked to consult with President George Bush on family related matters.

Dr. Dobson is married, the father of two children, and resides in Southern California.

If you would like to know more about Dr. James Dobson or Focus on the Family, please write to

Focus on the Family
801 Corporate Center Drive
Pomona, CA 91768